NAVIGATING *sexual love* IN CHRISTIAN MARRIAGE

A Playful Pursuit of Purpose

SCOTT BENNION

PRAISE FOR
NAVIGATING SEXUAL LOVE IN CHRISTIAN MARRIAGE

"*Navigating Sexual Love in Christian Marriage* is a wonderful addition to existing resources on marriage. Bennion has given Christian couples a true gift, providing a deeply biblical model that cuts through harmful extremes (the 'Radical No' of purity culture and the 'Radical Yes' of secular culture) while offering deep and practical insights. Christian couples wanting to experience deeper, healthier sexual intimacy will greatly benefit from this book."

—Steven Tracy, Ph.D.
Professor of Theology and Ethics, Phoenix Seminary (retired)
Founder and President, Mending the Soul Ministries

"Sacramental in character, Christian marriage engages the full embodiment of spouses, with the sexual dimension being integral to their shared love for each other, a participation in the communion of love that is the Triune God. Enlisting scripture and tradition, history and theology, and personal and pastoral experience, Scott Bennion offers in this brief, passionate book an opening for married couples to heal or enhance this crucial dimension of their mutual vocation."

—Bruce T. Morrill, S.J.
Edward A. Malloy Chair in Roman Catholic Studies
Divinity School, Vanderbilt University

"Christian marriage brings distinctive challenges to the already difficult task of addressing sexual desire, particularly where holiness has been imagined as incompatible with mature embodiment. When sexual desire is treated primarily as something to be feared or expelled, it distorts the self and inhibits a healthy appreciation of embodied personhood. Bennion's choice of the word 'navigating' is therefore especially apt: understood as part of the spiritual journey, sexual healing becomes not merely a problem to manage but a shared pilgrimage toward fuller communion in Christ. This book offers a humane and theologically grounded vision of marital sexuality as a demanding yet grace-filled dimension of Christian life."

—Dan Scott
Anglican Bishop (retired)

"Scott Bennion offers a wise and compassionate vision of sexual love that avoids both shame-based teaching and the 'anything goes' messages of our culture. Grounded in commitment, purpose, and faithful love lived out in real bodies and real lives, this book helps Christian couples see marital intimacy not as a problem to solve or a technique to master, but as a meaningful and life-shaping gift. Although the book does not always spell this out directly, it points toward the pattern of self-giving love revealed in Jesus Christ, a pattern husbands and wives are called to live out in their relationship with one another. Many readers will find in these pages a hopeful and much-needed alternative to the confusion surrounding sex and marriage today."

—Jonathan G. Smith, Ph.D.
Anglican Missionary Bishop, Reach Global Missions
President, Aidan University
President, Logos Global Network

"The Church in our times faces a particular challenge in confronting both the 'radical no' of purity culture and the 'radical yes' of sexual permissiveness. This is evident in marriage preparation, in pastoral counseling for couples, and as the Church guides parents in educating their children about the truth, beauty, and goodness of human sexuality. I am grateful for the work Scott Bennion has done, not only for the clear and straightforward way of naming the issues so many people across denominations are confronting, but even more for the personal testimony he offers, which is a reminder that *Navigating Sexual Love in Christian Marriage* is truly a work of personal healing and conversion. I pray that this text will both inspire and accompany readers as they embark on their own healing journeys."

—Rev. Sean Kilcawley, STL, PSAP-S

"This book offers a thoughtful, balanced, and deeply humane Christian framework for understanding sexual intimacy in marriage, moving beyond both shame-based purity culture and hollow permissiveness. Bennion integrates theology, clinical insight, and lived experience in a way that feels honest, compassionate, and grounded in real marital struggles. It is especially valuable for couples and clinicians seeking a purpose-driven, healing, and spiritually integrated vision of marital sexuality."

—Floyd Godfrey, Ph.D.
Clinical Sexologist
Certified Christian Counselor

"*Navigating Sexual Love in Christian Marriage* offers a compassionate and theologically rich path through one of the most tender areas of married life. Drawing from pastoral experience, personal brokenness, and deep sacramental vision, Scott Bennion invites couples to move beyond shame and cultural extremes into a healing understanding of intimacy as a place where God's grace meets embodied love. This book speaks with necessary honesty about wounds many carry in silence and gently reframes marital sexuality as a space of mutuality, dignity, and spiritual meaning. It is a hopeful, restorative guide for couples longing not just for better communication or technique, but for deeper communion with each other and with God."

—Scott Weeman
Founder, *Catholic in Recovery*
Author, *The Twelve Steps and the Sacraments*

"*Navigating Sexual Love in Christian Marriage* feels like discovering water in the desert. This book is an answer to prayer for Christians genuinely seeking to embrace a holy vision for marriage while also grasping for approaches that leave behind shaming scripts. Bennion's work is masterfully integrative of the wisdom from various Christian traditions, offering a holistic framework for marital intimacy that leaves room for the Holy Spirit to heal and transform hearts from the inside out. As a Catholic clinical psychologist who specializes in sexual development and Christian faith, this resource is one I am eager to be able to recommend wholeheartedly to married couples and single people alike!"

—Julia Sadusky, Psy.D.
Licensed Clinical Psychologist
Author of several books, including *Talking with Your Teen About Sex: A Practical Guide for Catholics*

"When a taboo-related topic shapes theological and pastoral care conversations, it often feels safer to avoid direct engagement. Dr. Scott Bennion's book, *Navigating Sexual Love in Christian Marriage*, addresses one such topic that many hesitate to confront, let alone publish a book about. For that reason, I deeply commend Dr. Bennion's bravery, vulnerability, humility, and authenticity in articulating his theological and pastoral care convictions to help those who have suffered in silence. Too many couples have carried traumatic pain because this subject has been suppressed, misunderstood, or ignored. Readers will find that Dr. Bennion shines light into a darkened space, offering sound theological reflection and compassionate pastoral care that speaks healing into places where Christian couples have wrestled with shame rather than experiencing the freedom and restoration God intends."

—Rev. Dr. Sanghoon Yoo, MSW
Founder, The Faithful City
Assistant Professor of Social Work, Huntington University

"*Navigating Sexual Love in Christian Marriage* provides guidance in offering a broader view of the role of sex in a couple's marital relationship. It does not offer 'how-tos' but rather encourages the Christian reader to explore new ways of thinking about their sexual relationship. *Navigating Sexual Love in Christian Marriage* would be helpful to Christian clergy and Spiritual Directors/Companions in their work with couples."

—Linda MacLeish, M.C., L.P.C.
Retired Mental Healthcare Executive

"Drawing on decades of experience, study, and prayer, Dr. Scott Bennion guides readers toward a deeper understanding of human sexuality, offering a careful and timely account rooted in the historic Christian vision of the profound spiritual connection expressed through both physical and emotional intimacy."

—Richard Lee, D.Min.
Commander, Chaplain Corps, U.S. Navy (retired)

"Bennion is able to dissolve the negativity of some Christians' beliefs about sex and help couples to fully embrace what it means to have a rich sexual life that enhances their spirituality."

—Steven E. Wales, M.C., L.P.C.
Diplomate of Sexuality Therapy

NAVIGATING
sexual love
IN CHRISTIAN MARRIAGE

A Playful Pursuit of Purpose

SCOTT BENNION

To Lisa Rose, my beloved—
faithful companion,
sacred partner,
and the truest reflection of God's love in my life;

whose love has taught me
the sacramental meaning of
grace, fidelity, and joy.

With my body, I thee worship,
and with my life, I give thanks to the one true God—Father, Son,
and Holy Spirit,
who joined us as one flesh in holy mystery.

"This is a great mystery, but I speak concerning Christ and the
Church."
— Ephesians 5:32

DISCLAIMER

This book explores sensitive topics related to faith and sexuality within specific religious contexts. The research on which it is based intended to gain insights into what keeps married couples in midlife from an experience of sexual wholeness, integrity, and flourishing.

As a clinical chaplain and faith-based pastoral counselor, I have had the privilege of working with survivors of abuse related to faith and sexuality, and I have gained valuable insights into their challenges. I, too, am a survivor of both spiritual and sexual abuse. While I understand that each survivor's experience is unique, I hold a degree of solidarity and empathy.

The material discussed herein may be emotionally triggering for some readers, especially those who have experienced such abuse. I encourage all readers to approach this content with discretion and empathy, recognizing its potential emotional impact. It is crucial to provide support and resources for survivors, and my research was conducted with a commitment to sensitivity, informed by both professional experience and a profound respect for the experiences of survivors.

CONTENTS

PREFACE

This book is written primarily for married couples—particularly those in or entering midlife—who identify with historic Christian orthodoxy and are seeking a deeper, more integrated understanding of sexual love within marriage. It critiques perspectives that either impose rigid restriction or offer unchecked permissiveness—what I describe as the *Radical No* and the *Radical Yes*. Neither extreme, I argue, adequately captures the depth, beauty, and purpose of sexual love as it was divinely intended. In response, I propose a sacramental teleology for the marital embrace—one that integrates embodiment, intimacy, and transcendence within God's design. By teleology, I mean an understanding of sexuality oriented toward purpose—toward what sexual love is ordered to and ultimately for—rather than reduced to technique, performance, or mere pleasure.[1]

Here, sexual love is neither a hedonistic pursuit nor a mere obligation; rather, it's a playful and purposeful gift, one that fosters mutual delight while offering a glimpse of the divine. By embracing this approach, couples can experience their physical union not only as an expression of love but as a sacramental encounter with Love itself, the Triune God, and a foretaste of the life to come.

This book is for those seeking a deeper, more meaningful vision of marital intimacy—one that harmonizes faith, desire, and divine purpose.

PART I. INTRODUCTION

For nearly my entire adult life, I've been married. Like many people, I've navigated the highs and lows inherent in marital unions. These experiences have encompassed exceptional moments and ordinary times. Both contribute significantly to the intrinsic beauty and transformative essence of marriage. Marriage, by its very nature, serves as both a sanctuary and a crucible.

Those who persevere and lean into the challenges that come with marriage, rather than succumbing to the allure of the grass being greener elsewhere, will discover the qualitative nature of this union. However, to be transparent and a bit candid, I must express that few experiences have been as emotionally painful for me as the realm of sexual love in married life. The giving and receiving of love in the marital embrace, often marked by fits and starts, becomes an intense journey as two individuals yearn deeply to be seen, heard, known, and loved in this most intimate of encounters.

Regrettably, my struggles aren't unique. In my capacity as a faith-centered pastoral counselor in private practice, as well as in the context of the marital counseling I do as a VA Medical Center chaplain, I've witnessed recurring patterns of relational and sexual brokenness, where spouses persistently miss connecting. There's a prevalent misconception, often fueled by messages from the church and broader culture, that the resolution lies in discovering the right technique or tool, which contributes to destructive outcomes. While this book is grounded in Christian anthropology and sacramental theology, I've written with accessibility in mind, aware that readers come from a range of ecclesial backgrounds and levels of theological formation.

In the pages that follow, I invite you to join me on a journey, which I begin by delving into my own experiences; this is followed by an analytical examination of what I perceive to be prevailing and destructive trends or undercurrents. Subsequently, I propose an alternative path forward. The overarching aim is to engage in *a playful pursuit of purpose*, inviting a reconsideration of prevalent notions about sexual love in marriage.[2]

1 | A PERSONAL JOURNEY: SETTING THE STAGE

As I think about my experience growing up in the Church of Jesus Christ of Latter-day Saints (LDS Church or Latter-day Saints), I remember spending my youth trying to *do* what was necessary to be right with God and stay right with God. Much of my youth was focused on looking a certain way and living a life largely guided or informed by a rigid moral imperative that distinguished Latter-day Saints from others.

This focus on externals seems akin to the guarding of exits and entrances highlighted in Mary Douglas's work on Leviticus, where she looked at the holiness codes related to food, sex, and skin diseases.[3] The maintenance of borders literally determined who was in and who was out, and the holiness codes seemed to reinforce this. Civilization, or being civilized, was about putting things in their proper place and keeping them there. It was believed that if things weren't kept in their proper place, chaos would ensue and, ultimately, death would result. I experienced a moralism in my LDS experience that was often focused more on what one should not do than what one ought to be doing. This seems similar to what Douglas described, about keeping things in the proper place while maintaining borders and order.

From my experience as a Latter-day Saint and my understanding of the culture and theology, the LDS Church places a lot of emphasis on personal effort and works for achieving personal salvation and exaltation. Outward obedience to the LDS Church's teachings was the way one was determined to be worthy (or not) of God's blessings, temporally and eternally. One of the LDS Church's scriptures, *The Book of Mormon*, says it this way: "… for we know that it is by grace that we are saved, *after* all we can do" (2 Nephi 25:23, emphasis added). In another place in the same book, it says: "Yea, come unto Christ, and be perfected in him, and deny yourselves of all ungodliness; and *if* ye shall deny yourselves of all ungodliness, and love God with all your might, mind and strength, *then* is his grace sufficient for you, that by his grace ye may be perfect in Christ …" (Moroni 10:32, emphasis added).[4] In another of the LDS Church's scriptures, the *Doctrine and Covenants*, Section 89 forbids the use of alcoholic drinks, tobacco, tea, and coffee in what's known as the Word of Wisdom.[5] Church teachings also place a high degree of emphasis on abstaining from sexual intimacy of any kind until marriage. There's a lot of focus on what I would call *thou-shalt-nots*. For many in the LDS Church, when their worth and, ultimately, their salvation are tied to performance, it leads to feelings of guilt, shame, and fear. Shame is, in my opinion, the most destructive. This was my experience, and though it isn't everyone's experience, it persists for many. It's also important to note that this reality has similar expressions in other non-LDS religious contexts. While my experience unfolded within a particular religious context, these dynamics—moral reductionism, anxiety around desire, and the displacement of formation by rule-keeping—appear across many Christian subcultures.

Although my experience in the LDS Church wasn't what's known as "purity culture" proper, it was my introduction to trying to live a certain way to appease—or please—God, as I sought to do the right thing. My youth was fraught with messages that induced shame, and I consistently had to deal with my guilt about failing to measure up to this external religious standard or the fear of being judged by others in the religious community. My shame could be

more accurately referred to as "sacramental shame." In the words of
Moon and Tobin:

> Sacramental shame is a form of religiously imbued chronic shame that gets distilled in many ... as a disposition. Dispositional shame, however it is cultivated, holds people in constant fear of being rejected or abandoned because of who they are, and causes immeasurable, sometimes fatal harm.[6]

I struggled to feel worthy of God's love because, for me, divine love was tied to *my* performance. As I look back at the many messages I received from church leaders and family members, I can now see how they were spiritually damaging and even abusive. I was always led to believe that if I had more faith, was more obedient, and sinned less, I would get the spiritual answers I so desperately longed for. Internalizing these messages gave rise to spiritual distress and an ongoing sense that something must be inherently wrong with me.

Years later, I would leave the LDS Church and become a Baptist after a profound conversion experience. I learned that salvation comes to us by God's grace alone, through faith in Jesus Christ and His death on the cross and subsequent resurrection, not by my own good works. In contrast to the faith of my youth, I was looking to Jesus and His righteousness, not my own. At the time, this gave me a lot of comfort, and it still does today. My shift from the LDS faith to Protestant Christianity was more than merely changing religions. It was an identity change, in that trusting in Jesus alone for eternal life provided me with a new life and identity as well as forgiveness of my sins and a right relationship with God.

I went on to pursue a theological education and was eventually ordained. Unfortunately, when I was confronted with my own private sins, and eventually a divorce, I was met with what I experienced as a punitive moralism not altogether different from my LDS upbringing. I was told by my ecclesiastical leader and bishop, a pastor to pastors, "Make your marriage work or have all your credentials pulled overnight." At this point, I found myself in an existential crisis of sorts, with an added sense of despair and loneliness as my circle of clergy colleagues gradually fell away—until, before I knew it, nearly all of them had disappeared. It wasn't until years later, in a forgiveness exercise, that I recalled just how traumatic this experience was, affecting my relationship with myself, others, and God.

In the aftermath of this experience with my bishop, I found myself wandering and alone, like a "sheep without a shepherd" (Matthew 9:36 ESV). This led to a distancing of myself from Christianity and the Church. I *put Jesus on the shelf*, so to speak; though I never denied my faith, I largely lived life on my terms like the prodigal son, experiencing even more relational and sexual brokenness while looking for love in a "far country" (Luke 15:13). I found myself exploring, studying, and living out permissive ideas and views related to relationships, sexuality, and spirituality that, in many respects, were the complete antithesis of both my upbringing as a Latter-day Saint and my Christian faith as an emerging adult.[7]

PART II. THE CULTURAL CONFLICT

2 | NAVIGATING EXTREMES: *RADICAL NO* AND *RADICAL YES*

In order to address relational and sexual brokenness, I focus on what I view as the *Radical No* and the *Radical Yes*.[8] One seems to be fueled by what's been called "purity culture," the other by what I think could be referred to as "permissive culture." I hope to show that although these two concepts may have had good intentions, they often keep Christian couples from experiencing an integrative and flourishing sexual life with one another and an intimate relationship with the Triune God.[9] Looking primarily at these two undercurrents in no way suggests that there are no other factors inhibiting sexual flourishing between couples (e.g., desire discrepancy, infidelity, lack of sex education, pornography use, trauma). It's also not to suggest that some might not already be able to navigate them successfully as people of faith. However, in my view, the impact of these two undercurrents is more dominant than often realized in the lives of Christian couples and relationships in the broader culture. By starting with the *Radical No* and the *Radical Yes*, I'm seeking to bring attention to what I believe may be driving forces of unhealthy sexual attitudes and behaviors, ultimately undermining sexual flourishing at a foundational level.

First, a word about other factors inhibiting sexual flourishing between couples. Couples rarely seek me out directly to help them with their sexual health and relationship. Rather, they often present as needing help with communicating better, or they're looking for help with increased conflict arising in their relationship. As therapists say, "the presenting issue is often not the issue." When I discover a lack of sexual flourishing in a couple's relationship, it often presents as some type of desire discrepancy or low sex/no sex (having sex less than once a month). Sadly, both partners come to counseling defeated, not as a unified front but often either pointing fingers at one another or with one party assuming full responsibility.

As we go deeper, unresolved issues such as pornography use, feelings of betrayal, infidelity, and trauma come to the surface. Sometimes, these issues are private, and sometimes, they're known. Further, it becomes clear that there are layers of guilt, shame, and a lack of sex education. Many couples have little to no shared vision or values regarding sexuality. Sexual flourishing is a foreign concept, and how sexual love contributes to the health of their relationship with each other and with God is equally foreign. Many couples have little to no consciously held personal principles that they hold individually. Typically, I introduce them to basic sexual health principles like:

1. Consent

2. Nonexploitation

3. Protection from HIV/STIs and unintended pregnancy

4. Honesty

5. Shared values

6. Mutual pleasure.[10]

Introducing individuals to principles associated with sexuality estab-lishes a foundation for further conversations on sexual values.

I acknowledge the mutual influence of physical and emotional intimacy. According to Christian authors Shaunti Feldhahn and Michael Sytsma, struggling couples have less sex, while thriving couples have more.[11] Prioritizing sexual intimacy in marriage is crucial. Before delving into its components, let's examine the *Radical No* and *Radical Yes* and their impact on the foundation of sexual love and flourishing.

3 | THE *RADICAL NO*: PURITY CULTURE

The first undercurrent I want to explore is what I call the *Radical No*, which has also been referred to as "purity culture," an evangelical movement that promoted a particular biblical interpretation and view of purity. Purity culture arose in the early 1990s, on the heels of a decade marked by the pain and uncertainty of the AIDS epidemic.[12] It lasted about a decade, but its effects are far-reaching. It was an effort to support young people in abstaining from sexual relations until marriage. Related to purity is the idea of holiness (or being set apart), but though purity is a part of holiness, when considered alone, it becomes truncated. Holiness appears to have a directional focus, a teleological purpose that involves being set apart for God. Being holy seems to mean living in accordance with whom you were created or designed to be as an image bearer of God. In the Anglican tradition in which I was shaped and ordained, purity is an expression of personal holiness that benefits one's relationship with God as well as with others in the community of faith. You can read more about this perspective of holiness from Anglican theologians such as J.I. Packer and John Stott.[13] They saw the pursuit of personal holiness as an essential aspect of spiritual growth and Christian witness.

Purity, on the other hand, as a goal in and of itself, seems to miss the deeper teleology of holiness and to be more about getting to a finish line of sorts. It's for this reason that I suggest it becomes truncated when considered alone. Sadly, I think this is often the result because many conversations about purity happen in isolation. What we need more of are sustained, honest conversations, conversations capable of bearing both vulnerability and truth[14]—for example, community offerings such as workshops with a sex-positive curriculum, not merely isolated private book studies where people are left to themselves to make sense of things. Though purity culture is not a Scriptural expression itself, Scripture does often reference leading a pure life, one that's set apart. Passages from the Bible, such as 1 Thessalonians 4:3–8, Romans 12:1, and 1 Corinthians 6:18–20, were used to support purity culture's position. For instance, the Apostle Paul writes to early Christians:

> For this is the will of God, your sanctification: that you abstain from sexual immorality; that each one of you know how to control his own body in holiness and honor, not in the passion of lust like the Gentiles who do not know God; that no one transgress and wrong his brother in this matter, because the Lord is an avenger in all these things, as we told you beforehand and solemnly warned you. For God has not called us for impurity, but in holiness. Therefore, whoever disregards this, disregards not man but God, who gives his Holy Spirit to you (1 Thess 4:3–8).

On the face of it, it seems completely reasonable that one would be seeking to align one's life with the teachings of Scripture in pursuit of a life that aligns with one's beliefs and values. The problem, as I see it, is when the pursuit becomes an end in and of itself and extra-biblical codes of purity are put into place.

Another problem is how, in the words of Rebecca Lemke, purity culture "allowed many parents to skirt the responsibility of discussing sex with their child while simultaneously believing that the issue was being addressed through 'role models' and purity events."[15] In other words, it points out the neglect of parental responsibility to "train up a child" (Proverbs 22:6) and the ancient declaration of faith in God and the ways of God as taught in Deuteronomy 6:4–9. I witness the effects of such views and neglect in my practice. Regularly, when I ask clients about their personal and shared sexual values, they look at me mystified, not quite sure what I mean. When I inquire about messages they received in their home life or at church, they pretty much all shrug their shoulders and say, "We didn't really talk about it." What they do know, they confess, is from para-church purity gatherings and, largely, from the internet.

The result is that many people, especially women, struggle to own their voice in marriage due to feeling a lack of safety, not being in touch with their feelings and needs, and a fear of rejection.[16] As such, they defer to their husbands' sexual needs at the expense of their own. In session, I often see clients who attach their sense of self and spiritual worth to their sexual history, a sexual history full of shame that has been largely informed by messages they received from purity culture. This shame, and their lack of education about who they are as sexual beings and what sexual love in marriage looks like, presents itself when they come to see me. They often turn to pornography to fill this gap, and the newly married husband and wife often receive one-dimensional, dangerous, and distorted messages about the sensitive sexual intimacies of sexual love.[17]

To further complicate things, these messages around purity are different for men and women, often in ways that oppress women, causing them to lose their voice. Women received messages idolizing virginity. Virginity became synonymous with purity and even replaced their primary identity in Christ. Sex outside of marriage was viewed as dirty and dangerous, something to be avoided at all costs. To arrive at marriage not being a virgin was deeply shameful and struck their sense of worth and value at its heart. As Rachel

Joy Welcher writes in *Talking Back to Purity Culture*, "a woman's worth rests not in her soul but between her legs."[18] As such, clients (men and women) have disclosed to me how they would develop work-around behaviors to explore sexual activities other than intercourse—a technical virginity of sorts—all the while telling themselves they were pure and still a virgin.

I remember when Josie, a middle-aged woman, came to see me with her husband for couples counseling.[19] She shared about how, after nearly 20 years of marriage, she struggled to feel connected to her husband and how sexual intimacy had all but vanished. When I explored this with them, it became clear that they'd had little to no sex education; the primary messages they'd received from their parents and their local parish were to stay pure and that God would be most pleased if they were to marry as virgins. This highlights the truncated view mentioned above, as well as how silence about sexuality sends its own messages.

Women also received messages that they were not as sexual as men, downplaying who they were sexually. If they were taught about sexuality at all, it was through the lens of male sexuality. For instance, when couples share with me in session about struggles with desire or desire discrepancy, I often see that instead of a wife's *responsive desire*[20] (common to most women and men in midlife and beyond) just being viewed as different from *spontaneous desire* (common to most men before midlife and some women), it was often looked at as a weak or inferior sex drive.[21] According to Barry and Emily McCarthy, "low sexual desire and desire discrepancies are the most common sexual problem couples bring to therapy."[22] However, most couples present with a nonsexual reason for needing counseling (e.g., communication issues, conflict resolution).

In addition, they were often simultaneously burdened with the responsibility of being the sexual gatekeepers of men who seemingly couldn't control themselves, with women being told to dress modestly and receiving conflicting messages like the need to be attractive but not too attractive. All of this absolved men, directly and indirectly, from exercising self-control, one aspect of the Fruit of the Spirit (Galatians 5:22–23).

This mindset often carries over into married life, where the internalized messages received by women become a one-way duty to serve their husband's sexual needs while denying or suppressing their own needs for emotional and sexual intimacy. Thus, many lose their voice and sense of place in married life and don't experience the joys of sexual love. If that weren't sad enough, these oppressive and often abusive messages are all too frequently reinforced by pastors who are uninformed, untrained, or immature in matters related to sexuality. Examples of such abusive pastoral messages can be found in the book *The Great Sex Rescue*.[23] The authors point out how such messages perpetuate a culture of victim blaming and shame while often keeping the victims from getting the help they need. All of this leads to an environment that doesn't foster sexual flourishing.

When these messages carry over into married life and the marital bed, instead of there being an expression of sexual love that's motivated by the words of Scripture, "submitting to one another out of reverence for Christ" (Ephesians 5:21), the result is the opposite of health and wholeness. The space between becomes one of self-centered attitudes and behaviors, sex becomes a kind of god, and each partner's perceived needs fuel a sort of battleground. Hearts become hard, and two people who vowed to live life together as one now find themselves strangers in a strange land. They increasingly turn inward and consider contingency plans in their private worlds in the event things don't work out. This is sometimes referred to as an "emotional divorce," where one or both partners have disengaged from one another.

I'm reminded of two veterans who came to see me: Julie and Gary, a couple in their early 40s, for whom sexual intimacy was a dreaded and rare encounter.[24] I paraphrase: Julie's rolling to the outside of the bed thinking, "Is he going to want *it* again tonight?" while Gary's simultaneously thinking, "Is she ever going to want it again?" So, either it's a battleground for winners and losers or both retreat to the edges, and the marriage bed becomes defiled. By "defiling the marriage bed," I draw on the biblical understanding that sex between married partners isn't considered sinful or impure by God, so long as it's consensual and within the covenantal bond of marriage.[25] When mutuality is lost and competition becomes central, the marriage bed can become defiled or unholy. In other words, the harmony and shared understanding between partners is disrupted, leading to potential negative consequences for the overall health of the relationship.

The messages men received from purity culture were different from those received by women, but they were just as destructive. Purity culture taught men to evaluate women largely through the lens of their sexuality and contributed to them developing a mindset that conflated virginity with purity. Such a mindset leads to men sizing women up based on externals. Rachel Joy Welcher notes that in a sex-saturated society, purity culture leads men to think of themselves as obsessed with sex, that they're *sex machines* or *lust machines*.[26] She goes on to point out that John Eldredge "believes that the reason men fall into lust is because their manhood has been repressed, damaged, and managed."[27] When men in my practice internalize such messaging, they often view themselves as victims, enslaved to their sexuality. They identify with their passions more than Christ, and purity culture tells them to fight harder to win the battle; meanwhile, consciously or unconsciously, they're led to see women's behavior as a big part of what causes their struggle to be pure.

It's common for counselors and therapists to see how these ingrained messages lead to clients' inability to integrate their sexual and spiritual selves.[28] This *Radical No*, expressed through distorted and harmful messages about sexual purity, leaves clients with little to no understanding of how to integrate their sexuality into their lives. As a result, they struggle to navigate their identity while single and to embrace a healthy, flourishing sexual relationship within marriage if they choose to marry. Then, years later, often during midlife or when they're approaching midlife, they struggle with physical and emotional intimacy, not quite sure what's happened. Worse yet, such struggles are wrapped in shame and often accompanied by traumatic events, past and present, as they try to figure things out by themselves.

The living out of received values that aren't consciously held, many of which come from the messaging of purity culture and the *Radical No,* is something I routinely see in my practice. To put it another way, this highlights the work of Mary Douglas mentioned above: couples are living out received sexual values that are focused on keeping things in their proper place to maintain borders and order related to sexuality.[29] Clients have little to no awareness of how this impacts or limits their ability to experience an integrative and flourishing sexual life or how this robs them of intimacy with each other and with God. I wish I could say these messages have only been internalized by my clients with evangelical Christian backgrounds. However, this isn't the case. I find that this purity mindset, this *Radical No,* is larger and transcends the walls of evangelicalism. Perhaps it was always a part of the broader culture but came to be codified in these unhealthy ways within parts of evangelicalism during this time.

4 | THE *RADICAL YES*: PERMISSIVE CULTURE[30]

Another undercurrent I encounter when couples come to see me to address relational and sexual brokenness is what I call the *Radical Yes* of permissive culture. Many hear the word "permissive" and immediately associate it with words like *promiscuous*, as in having many indiscriminate or casual sexual relations. Others associate it with *lasciviousness*, or unrestrained sexual behavior, or a habitual inclination to such behavior (lustfulness).[31] Though these often do flow from the *Radical Yes* of permissive culture, they're not the same. As a reminder, the word *permissive* is about granting permission and excessive freedom of behavior.[32] I think this is an important distinction because when couples grant themselves permission regarding sexuality, it empowers them to consider exploring new ways of thinking about sexuality and participating in sexual love together. For example, a couple who visited with me released a linear, performance-driven view of sex. Once they were open to permitting themselves to try something new, they were better prepared to receive the idea that sex was more akin to a smorgasbord of options for pleasure and connection that they could decide upon together. They were also ready to consider sexual intimacy from a holistic perspective versus merely a linear one. While this was a successful shift of openness, it's problematic or perhaps even dangerous when a permissive mindset becomes unfettered.

This permissive, *unfettered* mindset around sexuality, this *Radical*

Yes, is best articulated by one of the leading voices on sexuality and relationships. Articulating her view of sexual health and fulfillment at a workshop I attended, Gabriella Cordova taught that the best sex, or sexual liberation, means having sex with whom one wants (or as many people as one wants), when one wants, as often as one wants, in whatever way one wants, provided there's mutual consent and best practices are in place.[33] For her and the other facilitators at this event, consent was king (or queen), and one's desires were central. This differs from a perspective that acknowledges the undeniable pleasure of sex but doesn't consider pleasure as the primary goal of sexual activity; instead, pleasure serves as the incentive for participation.[34]

Some of the mindset that flows from this *Radical Yes* is the desire for autonomy, self-realization, and excessive freedom of behavior, or perhaps full liberation from the *Radical No*. One strong expression of this desire for autonomy, self-realization, and excessive freedom of behavior is what's known as the "sexual revolution." A mindset emerged in the 1960s and 1970s when traditional religious and cultural beliefs and values around sexuality and relationships were being challenged by the introduction of new ideas, or perhaps by ideas from another period that were now taking root. Examples include the emergence of highly effective and affordable birth control, no-fault divorce, and the legalization of abortion. Before the emergence of reliable contraception, most women didn't have sex until marriage.[35]

Though the sexual revolution was a significant part of this social movement of liberation, it wasn't just about sex and relationships. Traditional paths and ideas were being challenged by those advocating for concepts associated with the sexual revolution, and life as it was known was changing. Ideas about gender and roles were being questioned as well, and there were growing legal rights for women. For instance, until the passage of the Equal Credit Opportunity

Act in 1974, many banks denied women—especially married women—access to credit cards or loans without a husband's signature. All progressive movements have inherent strengths and weaknesses, and this period was no different. These ideas weren't new but rather were newly discovered ideas from the past (e.g., Greek thought and culture), as well as ideas that were coming to center stage with the influence of continental philosophy, liberal theology, and psychology.

Author Robert Bellah coined the term "expressive individualism," which is an underlying attitude among those embracing the *Radical Yes*. He defines it this way: "Expressive individualism holds that each person has a unique core of feeling and intuition that should unfold or be expressed if individuality is to be realized."[36] This seems to align well with what I call a humanistic, existential psycho-spirituality. For many, God and His commandments were no longer at the center of things when making decisions, but each person was left to determine right and wrong for themselves—to create their own existential reality. Others see this as "emerging from a radical individualism, in part perpetuated by conservative Christian free market capitalism, which prioritized market choice as consumption as an end in itself."[37] Expressive individualism is likely the result of both secularization and consumerism.

Throughout the 21st century, each decade appears to have had progressively relaxed sexual ethics, morals, and values compared with the preceding one. Individuals in my office, particularly those who came of age during the 1960s and 1970s, often reflect on these decades as a time of sexual liberation, commonly referred to as the sexual revolution or what I term the *Radical Yes*. Opinions on this period vary, with some viewing it as a pinnacle of moral decay while others see it as a progressive high point. Either way, it seems that things have only accelerated since these decades. Regardless of how one views this period, it has not been without effect on relationships and sexuality. This reveals that people are spiritually hungry for deeper purpose and meaning in their lives as well as a greater sense of pleasure, connection, and sustained intimacy with themselves and others, including the Mysterious Unknown.[38]

One example of this new permissive culture of sex and relationships, the *Radical Yes*, is what's known as "hook-up culture," seen on college campuses and beyond. To illustrate, some of my clients also experienced trauma within the *Radical Yes* as they engaged in hook-up culture. I'm thinking of Amy[39], a single mom of two, who shared how she regularly hooks up with men to fill the void in her life, compromising her values about waiting for commitment. Looking back now at her chosen pattern of behavior, she's traumatized by her choices. She tells me how sex has lost its meaning and how she feels deep shame and grieves her loss of self.

It's important to understand that hook-up culture and "hooking up" (or casual sex) are different. Some of my clients practice casual sex and sex outside of marriage. They tell me that, as college students, their friends often discouraged them from dating and relationships, rather encouraging them to hook up sexually with other students as just part of the college experience. I wonder if underneath this sentiment is what Donna Freitas references in her book *Sex and the Soul*:

> A lot of people come into college expecting to meet their husband or wife ... once you get here you realize that it is really just not that easy to do. Like, finding love just isn't that easy. Sex is probably a lot easier.—student at nonreligious private university"[40]

Perhaps this is the case for some, while for others, being away from home means they can live life on their terms. They can explore things they want and largely escape their parents' beliefs, morals, and values.

What a hook-up looks like varies and is ambiguous, but "the purpose of the hook-up ... is the opposite of ambiguous. The goal is 'fast, random, no-strings-attached sex.'"[41] The aim is to establish a kind of meaninglessness with a purpose that helps one move up in perceived social status. This is the idea of hook-up culture in contrast to hooking up. It's this hook-up cultural mindset, the associated risks, and the implications that Lisa Wade says make so many students unhappy.[42] In other words, casual sex doesn't deliver in terms of existential meaning, and what it does deliver is superficial and risky. I say risky because in hook-up culture, alcohol misuse is considered a first step, and with alcohol in the mix, consent is ambiguous.[43] Thus, students are more vulnerable to sexual assault, and many students allow themselves to participate in sexual behaviors they would ordinarily choose not to do.

For example, I regularly have female clients who report how they've felt "worn down or needled by their partners" in sexual encounters. When alcohol is involved, they report feeling greater vulnerability and that they've given in only to regret it later. The lack of sexual education in both purity culture and permissive culture allows a variety of unhealthy sexual behaviors to persist, even in married life. The question remains: is hook-up culture really liberating? Again, per Freitas:

> Hookup culture … is antifeminist through and
> through. Within hookup culture, the hookup is not
> an exciting, liberating sexual encounter that introduces participants to the freedom of unfettered sexuality and pleasure. Instead, young adults learn they
> have no choice but to accept—whether they like it or
> not—that the hookup is the norm for sexual intimacy. They learn that they must be casual about sex—
> even if they don't feel that way. They learn that sex is
> something you 'trade' for social acceptance; that sex
> is something to get done much like the dishes; and

that pleasure is low on the list of concerns, if it is there at all.[44]

Sexual liberation promises a lot, especially to women, by granting them a greater platform for their voices to be heard regarding roles and rights. However, it falls short in providing deeper levels of spiritual and existential meaning.[45] Further, it's not without consequences, both immediate and long-lasting, as revealed in my practice as a couple's counselor. This has been highlighted by the work of feminist author Louise Perry and journalist and opinion writer Christine Emba.[46] Permissive culture has a shadow side with mental health implications just as much as purity culture does.

Another example on the rise that lands within this area of the *Radical Yes* and the broader hook-up culture is consensual non-monogamy (CNM), a clinical umbrella term used to describe nontraditional, open relationship styles such as polyamory, monogamish, and swinging. Polyamory means many loves. It's the practice of, or desire for, romantic relationships with more than one partner at the same time. It prides itself on the informed consent of all partners involved.[47]

It was during my time "with Jesus on the shelf" that I embraced a polyamorous lifestyle. I encountered people who shared some of my values related to personal and relational growth, self-awareness, emotional intelligence, and open and honest communication. I leaned into what the permissive lifestyle offered and promised regarding relationships and sexuality. I learned and tried many different things, and the experience provided me with a lot of "fieldwork" as I interacted with others. However, though satisfying and even fun at times, polyamory and open relating added extra complexity to my life. There was even a season when I was involved with teaching in the community about conscious sexuality and relationships, and when I explored teachings from other schools of thought about the subject.[48] In these circles, sexuality is seen much like psychedelics: as a path to spiritual liberation.[49] It's important to note that it wasn't all about sex; however, "temple nights" were about leaning into edges emotionally and physically with sexual and nonsexual touch.

One client, Matt, confided in me that though there were no formal expectations at temple nights, he felt there was subtle but significant pressure. He owned that, in his own words, "it could be his own stuff," but his intuition told him he wasn't the only one feeling this way. We talked about how the environment seemed to break down one's convictions and sensibilities related to sexuality and relationships.[50] These "mystery schools" lean heavily on spiritual monism—a "mind alone is eternal" worldview (e.g., mystical Hinduism and Tantra, Gnosticism, the New Age, and various occult practices).[51] The rhetoric in these circles, including polyamory and sexual shamanism, was often about relationships and love.

Many were there not solely in pursuit of personal and spiritual growth but also to provide a sexual outlet for struggles in their monogamous relationship due to mismatched sexual desire.[52] Even though polyamorous proponents say this is not a reason to embrace polyamory, I regularly encounter people with this view in my practice. To be fair, even my wife and I have mismatched sexual desire, and this is common among heterosexual couples. I would argue that every couple has differences in desire. However, upon closer examination, dealing with differences in desire is more complex than merely connecting with a different partner.

It's common for me to meet with clients who are serial monogamists and ready to exit their current relationship, stating, "It just wasn't meant to be." The reality, though, was that the "love drugs" had worn off, meaning the honeymoon period had ended. To illustrate, Mitchell, a divorced father of three and an entrepreneur in his early 50s, sought me out for help with a "string of failed relationships."[53] From our time together, it became clear that somewhere between six and thirty-six months, around the time the honeymoon period ended, he would either end his relationships or sabotage them to bring about their end. In a sense, polyamory provided him with a place to medicate and feel good with serial relationships and sexual encounters, until reality set in. He lacked the skills, tools, and practices to lean into relationships where fulfillment and flourishing were to be found.

Whether in polyamorous or monogamous relationships, there's a point where the "love drugs" wear off and the relationship gets real. Permissive culture does its best to mask this, but in my experience, personally and professionally, it leaves one wanting and desiring more. It lacks theological and existential meaning and seems to fall short of the idea of freedom and liberation.

PART III. FINDING A BALANCED APPROACH

In this section, I aim to present a teleology for sexual wholeness, integrity, and flourishing, offering an alternative perspective to conventional notions that treat procreation, purity, and pleasure as ends in themselves. The objective is to address the paradox of hedonism, which suggests that individuals who consciously strive to maximize their personal pleasures are more prone to failure than those who prioritize intrinsic concerns for others and other entities.[54] This paradox suggests that focusing solely on personal pleasure can lead to greater challenges, while a genuine prioritization of others inherently contributes to more successful outcomes. This exploration aims to shed light on the complexities of, and the intricate interplay between, personal and communal well-being.

In practical terms, I intend to reconsider established ideas about sexual love and intimacy. This involves moving beyond the conventional emphasis on abstaining from sexual activity until marriage as the ultimate objective and dispelling the notion of sexual fulfillment as an isolated goal. Instead, the focus is on a nuanced understanding of intimacy, exploring what sexual flourishing entails for Christian couples in or approaching midlife within the context of marriage. Ultimately, I propose an alternative path that goes beyond the extremes of the *Radical No* and *Radical Yes*. This path aims to offer a conceptual framework, grounded in foundational elements, for understanding sexual love and the marital embrace[55] within the context of marriage. The framework is designed to resonate with couples, promote a deeper sense of embodiment, and foster intimacy with themselves, each other, and the Triune God.

From my time working with couples, it's clear that conversations about sex and sexual intimacy are often neglected. Whether Christian or non-Christian, many individuals enter married life ill-prepared, particularly in the realm of sexual intimacy. In the course of questioning couples about their sexual values, a recurring observation is the manifestation of perplexity in their responses: a state of surprise or being caught off guard, similar to the reaction of a deer in the headlights. What swiftly becomes apparent is that the values they do hold have been inherited from family, peer groups, religious leaders and church life, personal experiences, education, culture and society, media and entertainment (including pornography), and online communities and influencers. Their values generally come from a combination of these areas. Unfortunately, the prevalence of received values that are often unconsciously held aligns not only with my professional experience but also with the narratives I've encountered from individuals beyond the clinical setting.

Thus, people find themselves living according to values they haven't consciously embraced, all the while being significantly influenced by extremes such as the *Radical No* and *Radical Yes* mentioned earlier. The concept of an integrative approach to experiencing sexual flourishing within marriage, one that supports deeper levels of intimacy and connection, often remains distant and overlooked. Nevertheless, when I question clients about their motivations for engaging in sexual activity and what makes it appealing to them, the common thread, almost without exception, is the pursuit of shared pleasure and connection.

There's a noticeable absence of healthy sexual education and formation before marriage within orthodox Christian faith communities.[56] This deficiency tends to manifest later in married life, particularly during the midlife stage. As an illustration, women frequently disclose less than desirable, obligatory, or coercive early sexual experiences during counseling sessions, with such revelations often not occurring until midlife. Such experiences profoundly influence their sexual trajectory, often manifesting in conditions such as vaginismus and diminished desire. These findings underscore the enduring impact of early sexual encounters on women's sexual well-being, and they also emphasize the importance of addressing emotional aspects alongside physical concerns in fostering a healthy sexual journey for married couples.[57][58] They also underscore that not all sexual experiences are positive or conducive to health and that power imbalances can ultimately result in negative or unhealthy outcomes and even abuse.

Many of my clients express that engaging in theological discussions about sexual matters isn't a common practice within their families or congregations. Instead, there seems to be a prevailing culture of silence, leaving a void that's often filled in less than healthy ways. When families or churches seek to offer guidance on sexual formation, their approach often centers around advising what to avoid rather than having a discussion about the healthy aspects and the essence of sexual well-being. In simpler terms, these efforts often lack a comprehensive and constructive approach. In some cases, they can even be detrimental. This gap in sex education and a lack of open dialogue can lead to challenges in marital intimacy, leaving couples ill-equipped to navigate these issues effectively as they progress through their married lives.

Fortunately, within the landscape of orthodox Christian faith communities, there are some thoughtful and well-informed theological voices emerging that address the issue of sexual formation with depth and care. These individuals and resources offer valuable insights into navigating the intersection of faith and sexuality. They emphasize the importance of sexual integrity, flourishing, and fulfillment, supporting embodiment and intimacy for married couples, particularly during midlife.[59] Karol Wojtyla, a conservative-to-moderate thinker, explores the philosophical and ethical dimensions of love, emphasizing the importance of personal responsibility and self-giving in human relationships (expressed popularly as being a *good gift*). In his later work as Pope John Paul II, he further developed these ideas, presenting a profound theological exploration of the human body, sexuality, and the divine plan for the unity of man and woman in marriage. Both are works that one could spend a lifetime studying.[60]

By drawing from these theological sources, I hope to illuminate healthier approaches to sex education, fostering greater understanding, intimacy, and fulfillment in Christian marriages—especially as couples enter the midlife phase and beyond. These voices provide a unique perspective on cultivating a sense of sexual flourishing that not only aligns with one's faith but also enriches the marital experience, emphasizing the holistic development of a couple's physical and emotional connections.

Important to the theological and psychological exploration of sexual love within Christian marriage is a good understanding of historical developments of human sexuality. Throughout the history of Christianity, various theological voices have shaped attitudes toward sexuality, building on the notion discovered within the exchange of letters between the Apostle Paul and early believers in the Messiah, Jesus of Nazareth, that "… sexual morality was a presumptive requirement of communal belonging."[61] Representing the Eastern tradition, St. Gregory of Nyssa and St. Maximos the Confessor are regarded as emblematic figures. In the Western tradition, the influential presence of St. Augustine overwhelmingly shapes the landscape. Augustine's theological perspectives regarding marriage established a lasting basis for Western Christian teaching in this sphere for the subsequent fifteen centuries, and they continue to hold significant sway even in contemporary times.[62]

Both Eastern and Western traditions conclude that original sin casts sexual love within the sacrament of marriage in a less than favorable light.[63] In the words of Tatha Wiley, "The Christian doctrine of original sin has fallen on hard times. And it has been articulated in ways that seem to deny the goodness of human sexuality and even of being human."[64] Virginity came to be viewed as a superior path, and the legacy of early Christian asceticism, which emphasized celibacy and the renunciation of worldly desires (e.g., lust, concupiscence, etc.), is regarded as a path to spiritual purity.[65] This ascetic strain of thought often regarded the physical and sexual aspects of human life, and even sexual love within marriage, with suspicion, associating sexual acts with sin, temptation, and inferior or base aspects of humanity. This backdrop, combined with certain interpretations of biblical texts that highlighted sexual restraint, contributed to the perception of sexual love in marriage as inherently sinful, or at least problematic. In certain contexts, the idealization of virginity is associated with the notion of purity and the elevation of celibacy as a more spiritually elevated state.[66]

However, in the Eastern Orthodox tradition, there has been a somewhat more balanced approach in more recent years, where marriage as a sacred institution acknowledges the healthy aspects of sexual love while still advocating for self-control.[67] Even in the West, works such as Pope John Paul II's *Theology of the Body* seem to offer a fresh understanding of sexual love and the marital embrace within the institution of marriage that, in my opinion, challenges the theology of some of the Church Fathers and early writers.[68]

In more recent years, contemporary Christian theology and psychology have sought to revisit these historical viewpoints. They emphasize the sacredness of marital intimacy and encourage a more complete appreciation of sexual love within the context of a dedicated and affectionate covenant marriage.[69] These efforts align with the current and best insights from human psychology and relationships while staying true to orthodox Christian values. This endeavor seeks to emphasize and elevate the sacred nature of marital sexuality, recognizing it as a divinely ordained gift that plays a vital role in the spiritual and emotional connection between a husband and wife. This perspective highlights that the pursuit of holiness rather than mere personal happiness by spouses is a necessary component of covenant love expressed in sexual intimacy.[70]

5 | A NEW PATH BEYOND THE EXTREMES

When I counsel married couples on issues related to their sexual intimacy, they often mention their disparity in desire. They view this disparity as a form of sexual brokenness. As a clinician, this deeply saddens me because such a perspective often sets spouses against each other, hindering their ability to embrace a shared approach to sexual wholeness. This robs them not only of joy but also of the physical, physiological, psychological, and spiritual benefits of sexual love.

At its core, this struggle reveals a profound yearning in both partners—to be truly seen, heard, known, and loved in a way that fosters a deep sense of belonging and empowers them to live as fuller reflections of God. I suggest that this longing illustrates an essential aspect of sexual flourishing for Christian couples.

As I noted above, sexual flourishing could be related to keeping the marriage bed undefiled. Hebrews 13:4 states, "Let marriage be held in honor among all, and let the marriage bed be undefiled, for God will judge the sexually immoral and adulterous." This verse emphasizes the sacred and holy (or sanctified) nature of the marital union. In context, "the marriage bed" pertains to the physical closeness and intimate affection that's reserved exclusively for a husband and wife to partake of together in sexual love.[71] My theological interpretation understands "undefiled" as a sexual union that's considered pure and holy exclusively within the confines of a marriage. The marriage union, a sacred space, is thoughtfully designed by God for spouses to encounter intimacy, pleasure, and affirmation with one another, and it's not intended as a place for involvement with others. Within Holy Scripture, certain passages suggest that in the union of marriage, and through sexual love, one encounters a mystery that's both incarnational and transcendent. This offers a glimpse into the divine realm of union with God.[72] Here, in this playful encounter, time often seems to halt, creating a sacred moment.[73] Wife and husband seek to extend selfless love to one another as *good gifts*, opening the door to an embodied experience of oneness where two become one.[74]

Viewing the human body as a gift underscores the sacred nature of human sexuality and relationships. According to the theological foundations supporting this perspective, the body, including its sexual dimensions, is perceived as a divine gift, meant to be expressed and received with generosity and love within the sanctified covenant of marriage. This theological standpoint is enriched by the concept that love, as explored in St. Thomas Aquinas' examination of the nature of charity/caritas, involves the genuine pursuit of the well-being of the other.[75] In this sacred space, the realm of marriage, individuals can perceive themselves, their spouse, and God with renewed insight, fostering a connection that's profound, otherworldly, and rejuvenating. This perspective also magnifies God, as spouses, created in the divine image, strive to be gifts to one another. They do this through their presence and selfless love within the marital embrace. This mutual commitment enhances the sacredness of the marital bond, emphasizing reciprocity of presence and sacrificial love.[76]

It's because of what the undefiled marriage bed symbolizes, and how it points beyond itself, that the above passage undoubtedly suggests, and even seems to encourage, faithfulness—traditionally known as fidelity—within marriage and condemns adultery and sexual immorality outside of marriage. It underscores the crucial importance of upholding trustworthiness and commitment within the marital relationship, issuing a stern warning against infidelity and sexual sin.

This covenantal dynamic is embodied and sealed in the vows of matrimony, where each spouse promises "to have and to hold… for better, for worse, for richer, for poorer, in sickness and in health… till death us do part." In these promises, the Church hears not only human words of affection but also solemn oaths or vows made before God and witnesses that unite man and woman into a communion of life and love. The vows themselves protect fidelity, making visible the trustworthiness and permanence of Christ's covenant with His Bride, the Church. Therefore, Christian marriage is not just a private arrangement but a sacramental public witness to the world of God's faithfulness and love.

Grounded in Hebrews 13:4, this perspective is further enriched by theological insights and references from the New Testament, particularly Ephesians 5:21–33. In the context of "submitting to one another out of reverence for Christ," wives are called to submit to their husbands as unto the Lord.[77] Just as the church submits to Christ, wives are encouraged in this passage to submit, or voluntarily yield, to their husbands in everything. It must be acknowledged here that the phrase "in everything" doesn't imply absolutely every single thing. For instance, human depravity needs to be acknowledged, along with the conflicts that arise from competing loyalties, the need to submit to human authorities, and the imperative of obeying the Lordship of Christ.[78] Such a phrase must be understood in relation to the whole of Scripture, not as contradicting other clear teachings or principles that can be deduced from Scripture. For example, a husband insisting that his wife watch pornography with him during intimate moments is clearly against biblical teachings and should not be complied with.[79] This passage also emphasizes that husbands are called to love their wives sacrificially, following Christ's love for the Church as their example. It's this depth and quality of love that draws a heartfelt and embodied response from wives both within and beyond the marriage bed. This sacrificial love for one's spouse, as outlined in Scripture, is portrayed as sanctifying, purifying, nurturing, and cherishing. Reading the text carefully reveals that certain elements pertain to both husbands and wives, while others are exclusive to Christ's relationship with the Church.[80] The profound mystery of the two becoming one flesh, as stated, refers to the relationship between Christ and the Church. Consequently, the call is for each individual to love their spouse as they love themselves. This reflects Christian teaching that provides support for the sacred, sanctifying, and even sacramental nature of marriage.

Ephesians 5:21–33, viewed through the lens of sexual love in married life, reveals a theological and sacramental framework for understanding the marital relationship as a reflection of the divine union between Christ and the Church. The passage underscores the importance of mutual submission and selfless love between spouses, portraying sexual intimacy as a sacred and sacramental act of unity.[81][82] Lest it get overlooked, this *mutual* submission is highlighted in verse 21 of the passage. The husband's sacrificial love mirrors Christ's love for the Church, while the wife's respectful response mirrors the Church's devotion to Christ. Within the marital embrace, this dynamic plays out as a profound expression of spiritual and emotional oneness, where sexual love becomes a means of honoring and glorifying God through the harmonious relationship of husband and wife.[83]

Keeping this perspective in mind, I'd like to expand on the insights of modern Christian theology and psychology while also drawing from my understanding of the sacramental nature of relationships. This exploration reveals the marriage bed as a kind of sacred altar or, perhaps more accurately, restores the marriage bed as sacred. Such a perspective creates a space where sexual love in marriage is embraced, transforming it into a sacred realm for worship (or adoration) and profound reverence for one another, as both partners surrender together to the mystery that is God. Consider how this idea is captured in the way the word *worship* is defined in a work by Anthony LoBello:

> Worship Weekley says that the Anglo-Saxon noun *weorthscope* means *glory* or *dignity*; he points out that the word is equivalent to the combination *worth-ship*. It is a title of respect, as is clear from … the pledge in the old marriage ritual, "With my body I thee worship, and with all my worldly goods I thee endow," but now it is reserved for the appropriate attitude before the Almighty. In that regard, it is equivalent to the Latin *adoratio* and the Greek λατρεία.[84]

This helps to make sense of the eloquent words exchanged during the marriage ceremony, as presented in *The 1662 Book of Common Prayer*, which beautifully convey the commitment: "With this ring, I thee wed; with my body, I thee worship; and with all my worldly goods, I thee endow; in the name of the Father, and of the Son, and of the Holy Ghost. Amen."[85] What follows is a poetic interpretation of these words by American poet John Godfrey Saxe:

> That I adore thee, my most gracious queen,
>   More in my spirit than my body's sense
>   Of thine, were such incredible pretence
> As I would scorn to utter. Thou hast seen
> When eyes and lips, responsive to the heart,
>   Were bent in worship of thy lips and eyes,
>   Until, oh bliss! each pleasure-pulsing part
> Hath found its fellow in Love's sweet emprise;
>   Each answering other in such eager wise

As they would never cease to kiss and cling—
Ah! then meseemed amid the storm of sighs
I heard thy voice exclaiming, "O my King!
So may my soul be ever true to thine,
As with thy body thou dost worship mine!"[86]

This poem fervently expresses an authentic love, emphasizing shared moments of intimacy and a harmonious union of pleasures in the pursuit of a love that feels almost beyond reach. Godfrey hints at a mutual adoration that transcends mere physical sensations, delving into the profound depths of an ineffable, heavenly connection. There's also the suggestion of a reciprocal commitment between the individuals, extending to a shared realm that goes beyond themselves. The poem concludes with a resolute affirmation of unwavering commitment, intertwining the physical and spiritual dimensions of devotion inherent in a committed and enduring love.

The marital bed serves as a kind of altar, providing a sacred space for spouses to enter into the above and to forge deep connections with themselves, the Triune God, and their spouse. Here, husband and wife can express and exchange love, trust, and commitment in an embodied way that has the potential to shape all areas of their life together. Within this sacred context, the marriage bed transforms into a realm that offers an experience of intimate connection, shared pleasure, and affirmation as well as a place for healing and growth— and even a taste of transcendence.[87]

The marital bed stands as a distinctive space in which sexual love is revealed as a sacramental expression of the sacrament of marriage. It's important to clarify that this isn't to suggest that sexual love (or the marital embrace) is one of the seven sacraments found in either the Roman Catholic or Eastern Orthodox Church, which are available for everyone, but rather that sexual love is sacramental in nature.[88] Sexual love is considered sacramental in nature as it goes beyond the physical realm, signifying a sacred union that reflects divine principles and spiritual truths within the context of marriage, where the intimate connection between spouses becomes a tangible expression of profound unity and divine grace. Further, as mentioned above, this passionate and immersive bond of love between spouses mirrors the profound unity and intimate bond of love present in the sacred union between Christ and the Church. For this reason, it's not merely a bodily expression but a sacrament, a visible sign of an invisible reality, fostering a sense of reverence and sanctity within the context of the marital covenant.

6 | SEEING SEX AS SACRED: SACRAMENTAL THINKING

Sacramental thinking or imagination functions as a kind of lens, allowing us to see beyond what the physical eye can perceive.[89] My sacramental understanding is shaped partly by my formation and vocation as an Anglican minister. The Anglican view of the sacraments, deeply rooted in the idea that they're "outward and visible signs of an inward and spiritual grace," is expressed in the Anglican Catechism within *The 1662 Book of Common Prayer*.[90] It emphasizes the idea that the physical elements of the sacraments (for example, water in baptism, bread and wine in the Eucharist) are outward and visible signs that convey inward spiritual graces. In both Eastern Orthodoxy and Roman Catholicism, you see similar definitions. In simpler terms, a sacrament is (1) a sign, (2) given by Christ, which (3) imparts grace.[91]

The Anglican view of sacraments is similar to but different from the Roman Catholic and Eastern Orthodox perspectives. While many Anglicans, like Roman Catholics, recognize seven sacraments of the Church, there's some theological variation among Anglicans that allows for different interpretations, ranging from Evangelical Anglican to Anglo-Catholic. This variation exists because, although the Anglican tradition emphasizes Scripture, tradition, and reason, it lacks a living infallible interpreter. In contrast, Roman Catholic and Eastern Orthodox beliefs demonstrate a higher level of dogmatic precision (e.g., the Eucharist) and derive their authority from Holy

Scripture and Holy Tradition. This is even more strongly the case for the Catholic Church, with the Magisterium an infallible interpreter regarding faith and morals.

The Anglican view, for some, complements the Roman Catholic and Eastern Orthodox perspectives by offering a seemingly more inclusive approach situated between broader Protestantism and the ancient apostolic Church, sometimes referred to as the *Via Media*. It retains the seven sacraments but, according to the *Anglican 39 Articles of Religion*, distinguishes between Holy Baptism and the Lord's Supper, "two Sacraments ordained of Christ our Lord in the gospel," and the "five commonly called sacraments ... confirmation, penance, orders, matrimony, and extreme unction, are not to be counted for sacraments of the gospel."[92]

In a broader, non-church sense, a sacrament can be seen as a visible and tangible expression of sacred or divine realities within everyday life. A sacramental lifestyle involves recognizing and infusing daily experiences with deeper spiritual meaning, viewing them as opportunities to encounter the divine. In other words, seeing sacramentally reveals God through material existence. This broader understanding aligns with the Anglican definition of a sacrament, which often not only includes specific religious rituals but also emphasizes the sacred in the ordinary, recognizing God's grace at work through various aspects of life. Living a sacramental life means viewing and interacting with the world in a way that acknowledges and celebrates the presence of the sacred in everyday experiences.

With this in mind, sexual love within the sacrament of marriage serves as a powerful sacramental perspective through which to view it. The close bond shared between spouses becomes a visible and tangible symbol of a sacred reality woven into everyday life. Through the mutual exchange of love, trust, and commitment, the marital embrace takes on a sacramental nature, representing a deep unity that goes beyond the physical. In the context of a sacramental life, expressions of affection and intimacy within marriage are seen as more than just physical acts; they become channels for encountering the mystery that is God. They also guard against aspects such as purity, pleasure, and procreation—though important—becoming idolatrous ends in themselves. Furthermore, adopting this sacramental perspective urges individuals to approach their marital embrace with reverence. It encourages them to see it as an opportunity to both experience and express the sacred while also finding joy in the seemingly ordinary moments of playful intimacy or erotic playfulness within married life.

In the sacred tapestry that surrounds our existence as beings created in the image and likeness of God (Genesis 1:26–27), the ultimate destination we seek is revealed only in the divine presence of the Triune God. Every yearning, longing, aspiration, and desire finds its fulfillment in that holy presence. John 17:3 states it like this: "And this is eternal life, that they know you, the only true God, and Jesus Christ whom you have sent." This deep teleology emphasizes the core of human existence—to seek and know God. It's through pursuing this ultimate truth that the complexities of human relationships, especially the intimate bond of sexual love in marriage, gain a transcendent meaning.

When approached with understanding and reinforced by a complete and embodied marital embrace, sexual love becomes a gateway for experiencing the divine and getting a foretaste of the heavenly or Beatific Vision. In the words of Sean McDowell, "Sexual union on earth is a pointer, an anticipation, a foreshadowing of a deeper union we will experience in heaven."[93] According to Hans Boersma, author of *Seeing God*, the Beatific Vision is considered the highest and most complete state of happiness, surpassing any earthly joy or fulfillment. It's commonly associated with the idea of eternal life and viewed as the peak of the soul's journey toward God.[94] Within Christian theology, especially in Catholicism, the Beatific Vision is closely linked to the concept of theosis or divinization, where believers, by grace, share in the divine essence through the transformative process of salvation.[95]

I suggest that in the sacred bond of marriage, lovers catch a glimpse of the Beatific (or heavenly) Vision and the eternal love of the Triune God—Father, Son, and Holy Spirit. This idea of the Beatific Vision is rooted in passages like 1 Corinthians 13:12: "For now we see in a mirror dimly, but then face to face. Now I know in part; then I shall know fully, even as I have been fully known." The shared intimacy between spouses, naked and unashamed, becomes a window into this heavenly vision, reflected in the face of another—each an image bearer of the divine. This revelation unfolds in the vulnerable exchange of intimacy, pleasure, and affirmation of another, revealing that such joys are ultimately found in the Triune God and accessed through the redemptive grace in the person and work of Jesus Christ alone. All of this highlights the profound beauty to be found in the mystery of marriage and the marital embrace. It reveals a unique, sacred, and deeply human connection that both is beautiful and sacramentally points beyond itself.

To put it another way, this profound encounter isn't meant to be an end in itself. Instead, it acts as a catalyst for a higher calling. In the words of Christopher West, "The union of the sexes—as beautiful and wonderful as it is in the divine plan—it is only a faint glimmer, a pale picture within time of the eternal union with God."[96] From this sacred place of union, a transformative journey begins—a pilgrimage of two souls walking side by side with the pursuit of God at the center. Spouses embark on a shared mission, free from distractions that could hinder the path. Together, they prioritize not only the sanctity of their sexual union but also the greater pursuit of communion with the Triune God. Their intertwined lives become a testimony to the sacred dance of prioritizing the eternal over the temporal as they walk each other home to heaven. In this shared pursuit, the ordinary becomes extraordinary, and the mundane becomes a sacred rhythm of seeking God at every step of the journey.[97]

Moving from the profound and mysterious nature of sacred connection in marriage that's embedded in us, written in our very bodies, we now turn our attention to how to live out this vision. In the pages ahead, we'll examine key elements and practical steps to bring this purpose and its sacred values into everyday life. Essentially, this is where theory meets daily living and where the sacred intersects with the practical.

PART IV. PRACTICAL GUIDANCE FOR CHRISTIAN COUPLES

In the previous section, a sacramental teleology of sexual love was proposed as an alternative to what I defined as the *Radical No* and *Radical Yes*. It emphasized that the absence of a foundation like a sacramental teleology of sexual love allows elements such as purity, pleasure, and procreation—significant as they are—to become idolatrous ends in themselves.

The focus now shifts from the contemplative to the practical realm of the marital embrace. The aim is to make the theology discussed earlier accessible in everyday life, progressing from foundational principles to tangible steps and strategic suggestions. These are essential for spouses to fully experience the richness of their most intimate moments together. The upcoming pages serve as a template, guiding you through a transformative landscape where the sacred principles uncovered seamlessly integrate with the practical aspects of daily existence. This marks the point where theological foundations and practical components converge, allowing the spiritual aspirations of the sacred union or bond to find expression in an everyday theology of deliberate choices related to sexual love, made within the context of marital life.

7 | REDISCOVERING PURPOSE IN PLAYFUL INTIMACY

The subtitle of this book is *A Playful Pursuit of Purpose.* I wrote this section with that subtitle in mind because all too often, in sessions with clients and in the therapeutic context in general, attitudes about sexuality in particular are so serious that they undermine the playful nature of sexuality that's possible within marriage. This isn't to suggest that marriage isn't a serious relationship, nor is it referring to the seriousness of sexual encounters that are marked by a deep emotional and physical connection between partners; rather, it refers to the seriousness that seems to be a cover-up for emotional and existential pain. In married life, it's essential to balance the sincerity required for emotional and existential depth with the lightness of a playful friendship and laughter. Such an authentic connection goes beyond the seriousness that may serve as a mask for underlying pain. Thus, the subtitle, *A Playful Pursuit of Purpose,* seeks to provide a perspective for approaching this section and the marital embrace. It underscores the inherent playfulness that can be infused into sexual love, guiding the pursuit toward a deeper heavenly purpose.

Playfulness introduces an element of fun and enjoyment into married life. When spouses are willing to engage in playful exploration, they create a lighter atmosphere that can alleviate stress and create a sense of joy. Then, *erotic playfulness* in the marital embrace serves as a natural extension of the balanced dynamics in married life.[98] Erotic playfulness acts as a catalyst, fostering deeper levels of mutual understanding and intimacy. This, in turn, supports the sincerity required for emotional and existential depth, ultimately leading to a more profound shared pleasure and connection between spouses. Such playfulness allows for variety in sexual encounters, encouraging couples to try new things and break away from routine. Importantly, from my clinical experience, the element of communication is enhanced through playfulness, as partners feel more comfortable expressing desires and sharing what they find mutually pleasurable.

This kind of open, embodied dialogue—meaning the shared, honest communication that engages both the emotional and physical dimensions of the marital embrace and allows spouses to meet one another with their whole selves—develops through erotic playfulness and becomes a doorway to deeper understanding between spouses. As couples share honestly about what they enjoy, what feels meaningful, and where they sense vulnerability or hesitation, they come to know one another more truthfully as persons made in the image of God. In this sense, communication within the marital embrace isn't merely functional; it's formative. It helps each spouse perceive the other with greater tenderness and reverence, and it creates space for the couple to encounter something of God's own relational nature, which is Communion and Love.[99] At the same time, this embodied dialogue provides practical insight into each partner's desires, preferences, and emotional rhythms. Such knowledge contributes to a more satisfying and fulfilling sexual relationship, one that honors both the playful dimension of married love and its orientation toward a profound, sacred mystery.

8 | FOCUSING ON PURPOSE, NOT JUST TECHNIQUES

Techniques can only take one so far. What's truly needed is everyday theology, also known as practical theology. Being a *good gift* is less about reaching a specific benchmark and more about cultivating a disposition of mind, heart, and will that embodies sensitivity and consideration not just for oneself. As mentioned above, echoing the words of Saint Thomas Aquinas, it involves willing the good of the other.[100] With such a disposition and sensitivity, one can hold the other in whatever challenges they may be facing, whether it's the "gremlins" of trauma or simply the vicissitudes of life that impact the marital embrace.[101] Keeping this in mind, being a good gift and experiencing fulfilling intimacy can harmoniously coexist.

This invites one to make a pivotal shift, perhaps for the first time, toward embracing a theological perspective on sex that opposes male-dominated views of sexuality and performance models. It also dismisses the idea that sex is solely about pleasure without any profound existential or theological purpose. This necessitates the ability to cultivate a new understanding of sexuality that captures one's imagination. Simultaneously, it involves challenging destructive and self-defeating narratives from the past, as well as addressing the behaviors or patterns that result from those narratives.

Having a theological foundation that incorporates a sacramental lens of sexual love offers spouses a way to address the above without getting lost in the pursuit of purity, pleasure, and procreation as ends in themselves. This well-rounded understanding provides a pathway to integrate faith and sexuality. It informs and enriches intimate lives, ultimately leading to greater fulfillment and connection with oneself, each other, and the Triune God. Yes, procreation, purity, and pleasure matter and are a part of God's design for sexual love in married life. They also inform what it means to live from that design, but they point beyond themselves.

The marital embrace of sexual love is designed by God to be a beautiful, pleasurable, and expansive experience. It's a deeply connecting encounter of union and belonging that provides a foretaste, in the present, of the fullness of eternal life. This extends until the consummation of all things in heaven with the Triune God.[102] When spouses willingly and with a sense of curiosity adhere to this teleological vision of sexual love in marriage, and reject or at least temporarily suspend their narratives associated with the *Radical No* and *Radical Yes*, we can then explore practical approaches to educate and support couples in embodying this sacramental mystery. This involves implementing these ideas and transitioning from a performance or stair-step model of sex, akin to taking an escalator, to one that's mutual, deeper, and richer, resembling more closely a smorgasbord of delightful foods. In other words, spouses, as friends and lovers, embark on a shared pursuit of oneness, not merely orgasm.[103] Together, they create a sacred space that's expansive and supports the giving and receiving of love in a cyclical way, as opposed to an approach that's linear and purely goal-driven.

9 | ENJOYING RIGHTLY: PLEASURE IN LIGHT OF PURPOSE

Transitioning away from theoretical foundations, a mindset shift becomes imperative in the exploration of purpose-guided pleasure. Rather than viewing sex solely as a biological act, couples must undergo a transformative shift in perception. This paradigm shift involves spouses recognizing that their sexuality isn't a source of shame or a curse but rather a gift from God meant to be joyfully embraced. Despite the messages of the *Radical No* and *Radical Yes*, they'll need to intentionally embrace the concept that sexual love in marriage possesses a sacramental quality with deep teleological significance. Spouses may encounter resistance to this idea. This perceived challenge is an invitation for individuals to engage their imagination and to consider that the connection between sex and spirit may be closer than initially thought.

By allowing for such a shift, couples will be better prepared to begin looking honestly at letting go of or unlearning harmful messages related to sexuality, many of which are shame-based. No doubt, this work can be challenging and is often filled with complexity; for this reason, individuals may need the support of a pastoral counselor or Christian therapist with training in sexuality. From here, I hope that couples will be better prepared for practices and rituals that support an erotic playfulness conducive to teleology rather than mere techniques. The goal is to cultivate a form of intimate connection that goes beyond the physical—a connection that fosters soul-touching sex, which, in the words of Tim Gardner, "touches the deep yearning of the soul."[104]

Moving forward, I assume that couples have devoted themselves to the essential mindset work mentioned above. With this new perspective, we're now ready to transition to the practical application of these principles—what I like to think of as best practices and rituals.[105] I hope that couples will see, in the words of Rich Villodas, that "at the core of this relationship between sexuality and spirituality there is desire and longing" and "what we do with our sexual desires and longings says a lot about what we believe about God."[106] The following definitions for *spirituality* and *sexuality* from Debra Hirsh highlight this core desire and longing, which she calls "two sides of the one coin":

> *Spirituality* can be described as a vast longing that drives us beyond ourselves in an attempt to connect with, to probe and to understand our world. And beyond that, it is the inner compulsion to connect with the Eternal Other, which is God. *Essentially, it is a longing to know and be known by God (on physical, emotional, psychological, and spiritual levels).*

> *Sexuality* can be described as the deep desire and longing that drives us beyond ourselves in an attempt to connect with, to understand, that which is other than ourselves. Essentially, it is a longing to know and be known by other people (on physical, emotional, psychological, and spiritual levels).[107]

In my clinical experience, couples frequently connect with the idea that, at a profound level, we all share an existential need to be seen, heard, known, and loved.

These practices, ordinary as they may seem to some, extend an invitation for spouses to approach the marriage bed with a fresh perspective. It encourages them to embrace one another through their sexuality as meaningful gifts, trusting that their desires and longings will be fulfilled by something beyond themselves. The following are examples of a few practices and rituals designed to help spouses embrace the divine call to self-giving within the context of sexual love. These practices foster an "I–Thou" relationship, as Rudolf Otto calls it, marked by genuine interest in each other as bearers of the divine image.[108]

10 | INTEGRATING THE SACRED AND PHYSICAL

Having already recognized the marriage bed as sacred, serving as a kind of altar, there's no theological reason to exclude it from reverence. Couples are therefore encouraged to seek God's blessing upon their sexual life, both generally and in the particular moments when they come together in bodily intimacy. Such prayer is meant not to spiritualize away the physical but to consecrate it, reminding spouses that their union is an expression of covenantal love marked by vulnerability, fidelity, and self-gift. In this way, sexual intimacy becomes not merely permissible but purposeful, an embodied participation in communion with one another and with the Triune God.

This prayerful orientation need not be elaborate. It may take the form of simple intentions, petitions, or a silent acknowledgment of God's presence. What matters is the posture of intentionality. Far from interrupting intimacy, a brief pause to consecrate the moment sets it apart from the pressures of daily life and affirms that this aspect of marriage is worthy of care, preparation, and reverence. As experienced couples recognize, scheduling intimate time isn't a failure of spontaneity but an act of prioritization; prayer similarly marks this time as meaningful rather than incidental.

Alongside prayer, couples may benefit from intentionally creating a sacred space before engaging in intimacy or even in difficult conversations. Facing one another, placing hands on the heart, holding hands, maintaining eye contact, and touching foreheads while breathing together helps regulate the nervous system and foster presence. Some couples find it helpful to symbolically mark this shared space—imagining a boundary that holds their time together—before openly sharing desires, fears, boundaries, and hopes. Naming what they wish to invite, such as playfulness or creativity, and what they wish to set aside, such as fear or distraction, further prepares the ground for a meaningful encounter.[109]

From this explicitly prayerful framework, couples may then be introduced to practices that appear less overtly spiritual yet remain deeply integrative of body and spirit. These practices prioritize presence, consent, and mutual attunement, creating space for spouses to explore needs, values, longings, and desires together. Rather than emphasizing technique or performance, they cultivate an embodied encounter marked by interconnectedness and meaning, favoring teleology over utility and gift over grasping. These practices are grounded in the conviction that marital intimacy is not a matter of one spouse giving while the other merely receives, but a shared exchange in which both giving and receiving become expressions of mutual self-gift. This posture of mutual self-gift resonates with an understanding of marriage that favors radical generosity over strict notions of fairness, inviting spouses to give freely rather than measure love by equal exchange.[110]

One such practice employs a simple, time-limited structure that invites partners to take turns expressing how they would enjoy offering or receiving touch. The emphasis is placed on giving rather than taking, on clarity rather than assumption, and on consent rather than entitlement. By slowing down and limiting the duration, this practice creates a sense of safety in which trust can grow. Participants are encouraged to begin conservatively, avoiding sensitive areas, and to modify or discontinue the practice at any time. When approached with patience and attentiveness, such exercises often foster healing, deepen trust, and strengthen intimacy.[111]

In a complementary way, couples are invited to adopt a broader mindset toward sexual intimacy, one that reframes it not as a task, a mere obligation, or a measure of performance but as a shared hobby. This perspective asks spouses to consider how they think about sex and whether it holds a prioritized place in their lives together. Like any meaningful hobby, sexual intimacy benefits from curiosity, learning, intentional planning, and a balance of seriousness and playfulness. When treated as a hobby, the marital embrace becomes an arena for exploration rather than evaluation and for mutual enjoyment rather than competition.[112]

Reframing sex in this way encourages spouses to plan for intimacy, invest in education, attend to physical comfort, and communicate regularly about what's working and what isn't. Just as hobbies require time, resources, and periodic reassessment, so too does sexual intimacy flourish when it's treated as worthy of attention and care. The aim isn't indulgence but mutual delight ordered toward communion.

Together, these prayerful orientations, embodied practices, and attitudinal shifts help couples approach the marriage bed not as a place of demand or anxiety but as a sacred space of self-gift. In doing so, spouses are invited into an integration of sexuality and spirituality that honors the body, safeguards mutuality, and opens their love to transcendence.

11 | EMBRACING HEALING VERSUS ONLY SEEKING SOLUTIONS

Married couples, despite their genuine commitment and openness to embracing a new paradigm, may find that their experience of sexual love appears tepid or lackluster. They may even find themselves beset by challenges such as the following, some of which may come from unconsciously held core beliefs and others from common dynamics in marriage, and all of which I see in my counseling practice:

> Deep-seated limiting beliefs that may hinder a healthy view of sexuality

> Feelings of shame associated with one's sexuality

> Psychological and/or spiritual barriers or strongholds that impede a positive approach to intimacy, sexual wholeness, and flourishing

> Destructive messages that may have shaped one's perception of sex and relationships

> Trauma and associated triggers that may affect current sexual experiences

Lack of understanding about arousal and the nuances between responsive (or receptive) and spontaneous (or initiating) desire

Spouses with different levels of sexual desire, or desire seems absent

Not considering the balance between novelty and routine in maintaining a healthy and satisfying sexual relationship

Deeply rooted issues and specific challenges, some of which stem from the *Radical No* of purity culture and/or the *Radical Yes* of permissive culture, will likely arise in the context of the marital embrace. Furthermore, when spouses contemplate the profound teleology for which the marriage bed serves and the significance it holds, it should come as no surprise that the marriage bed is a battleground for spiritual warfare (Eph. 6:12). We're not merely addressing psychological dynamics.

With this in mind, let's explore a subtle but significant distinction between healing and curing in the context of the marriage bed. This differentiation is derived from the work of Bruce Morrill, who defines curing and healing as follows:

> *Cure* refers to the effective control or removal of the disease in a person's body. *Healing*, on the other hand, is an intervention affecting an illness. To heal somebody is to bring personal or social meaning to the misfortune experienced in illness such that the person attains a new or renewed sense of value and purpose in his or her world.[113]

As couples present themselves fully, with a sense of presence as gifts to each other, creating the potential for a profound connection that transcends the physical and delves into the realm of the eternal other, God, they should be aware that challenges such as those mentioned above will emerge. Even when couples adopt this renewed mindset and align themselves with the presented paradigm, challenges may still arise, potentially obstructing the sanctity of this sacramental space. It's not uncommon for a prevailing *curing* mindset to insist on a quick fix by resolving, managing, or eliminating various issues before the marital embrace can be mutually enjoyed.

This mindset emphasizes the importance of cultivating a nuanced understanding of intimacy, recognizing that the journey toward a fulfilling sexual connection, sexual wholeness, and overall flourishing requires ongoing exploration and acceptance rather than rigid adherence to a checklist of prerequisites. It encourages spouses to navigate challenges together, slowing down when necessary. While some traumas may persist, this approach views intimacy as a means of healing rather than a cure. This perspective underscores the need for sustained investment in each other and advocates for seeking professional help and resources when needed.[114] Furthermore, it challenges spouses to perceive encountering difficulties not as a sign of inherent issues but as an integral part of living in a flawed world. Ultimately, this mindset is rooted in the concept of *healing*, promoting growth and resilience in the face of challenges.

In essence, the proposed paradigm shift from curing to healing encourages married couples not only to change their actions related to sexual love but also to cultivate a mindset that values the journey of intimate connection as a continuous and evolving experience versus merely a destination or a problem to be fixed. Together, spouses celebrate and mourn the highs and lows of married life, including those that arise in the marriage bed. This approach fosters an environment in which spouses can navigate challenges together, embracing the depth and complexity of their shared journey toward a more profound and fulfilling union.

12 | FINAL REFLECTIONS AND ENCOURAGEMENT[115]

I embarked on a profound exploration of the multifaceted nature of sexual love in marriage, aiming to unravel its inherent mystery. Within the sacred covenant of marriage, I have discerned the essence of oneness. This unity is a profound connection that transcends the physical realm and delves into the depths of the supernatural, spiritual realm. When spouses come together as image bearers, they seek to be good gifts to one another, willing the good of the other.

To paraphrase *Theology of the Body*, such sexual intimacy between spouses flows from the four characteristics of authentic marital love. One that is *free* (consensual, not compelled or coerced), *total* (vulnerable and self-giving), *faithful* (an exclusive committed covenant), and *fruitful* (open to life, deeper connection, and ongoing growth in holiness).

From personal experiences, influenced by encounters with the *Radical No* and *Radical Yes*, I offer a path not as a distant observer but as an active participant. Through personal struggle and reflection, I've gained insights into the intricate interplay of human sexuality and spirituality. In navigating the extremes of denial and excess—either trying to suppress sexuality or being consumed and driven by it—I've reconstructed my narrative surrounding sexuality and the marital embrace.

Among the misleading choices regarding sexual love today, I find the *Radical No* and *Radical Yes* especially harmful to married couples. While there are elements to be learned from both extremes, this work sheds light on an alternative path—a sacramental teleology—that transcends the mere pursuit of purity, pleasure, or procreation as ends in themselves.

This journey of self-discovery has reshaped my understanding of sexuality and marriage. It has added a new dimension to my personal life, my marriage, and my vocation as a clinical chaplain and pastoral counselor. This work aims to guide others on similar journeys of personal and spiritual growth related to faith, love, and sexuality.

Appendix 3 outlines an approach to the next steps you can take to explore themes from this book, unraveling the complexities of sexuality as a formative spiritual experience within marriage, one where spouses can be *naked and unashamed*. Through ongoing shame-free conversations, let us be curious and open our hearts to love. As we do, we can grow in our understanding of sexual intimacy's transformative power to offer us a profound encounter and connection with the Triune God, each other, and ourselves.

AFTERWORD

This project began as a doctoral journey, but it quickly became something far more personal. I set out to explore the integration of faith and mental health because, in my work as a chaplain and pastoral counselor, I kept encountering a familiar fracture. People of deep faith were often suffering quietly, unsure how their spiritual convictions related to their emotional lives, their bodies, or their sexuality. Others had done the opposite—embracing therapeutic language and insight while quietly setting faith aside. I wanted to understand whether these worlds truly belonged together, or whether the divide we experience is something we've learned rather than something inevitable.

Along the way, this work became a sustained reflection on sexuality, sexual love, and marriage, not as isolated topics but as places where theology, psychology, embodiment, desire, and suffering all converge. Sexuality, I came to see more clearly, is never merely about sex. It's about belonging, vulnerability, trust, power, pleasure, shame, and hope. It's about what we believe, often unconsciously, about God, about ourselves, and about one another. My hope in writing was not to resolve every tension but to contribute thoughtfully and pastorally to an ongoing conversation that many couples struggle to have, or are having quietly, often without language or guidance.

Partway through the process of writing my doctoral thesis, my own body demanded attention in a way I couldn't ignore. I learned that I had significant heart disease. That diagnosis slowed me down, forced me to listen differently, and confronted me with my own fragility. It was no longer possible to write or think abstractly about embodiment, vulnerability, or limits. I was living them. The questions I was asking of others, about trust, surrender, dependence, and healing, were now questions I had to answer myself.

If that weren't enough, the seasons that followed my graduation carried further weight. As I began the work of transforming my thesis into a book, I entered the Catholic Church after a long and prayerful journey. Not long after, my body again asked for attention, this time through a bout of cancer, providing an opportunity for deeper interior work, an invitation to lean into family and friends, and a reorientation toward what matters most. Each of these experiences, along with a pilgrimage to Rome and Assisi for veterans focused on hope and healing during the Jubilee of Hope, reshaped me. They clarified some convictions and softened others. They deepened my sacramental imagination and refined my understanding of suffering, grace, and hope. They also made it unmistakably clear that this work was unfinished, not because it was inadequate but because life itself continues to unfold.

Looking back, I can say with confidence that I would write parts of this book differently today. Not because I disagree with what I've written, but because experience continues to teach me. I suspect I now have more to say about marriage, about sexual love, about healing, about the Church, and about the slow work of integration than I did when this project first began. But that will have to wait for another day

For now, I offer these pages as a faithful step along the way, an honest attempt to name what I've seen, lived, and learned thus far. If this work helps couples feel less alone, less ashamed, or more hopeful—if it invites deeper reverence for the body, for marriage, and for God's presence in the ordinary and the intimate—then it has served its purpose. The conversation continues. And so does the journey.

APPENDIX 1

A FINAL BLESSING: A BENEDICTION FOR COUPLES

May Almighty God continue to stir within us reverence and reflection for the profound journey we have undertaken—an exploration of the many facets of marital love within the Christian faith. Within the sacred covenant of marriage, may we discover anew the mystery of oneness: a unity that mirrors the divine communion between Christ and His Church, transcending the merely physical and opening us to the depths of the spiritual life.

As we reflect on our encounters with the *Radical No* and the *Radical Yes*, may we walk this path not as distant observers but as willing participants in God's redemptive design for our union. Through the intricate and holy interplay of human sexuality and spirituality, may we learn to navigate the extremes of denial and excess, guided by the teachings of Christ and the wisdom of Holy Scripture and Sacred Tradition. In doing so, may our stories about sexuality and the marital embrace be healed, redeemed, and rightly ordered.

Grant us the grace to recognize the harm of false choices and the courage to embrace an alternative way—a sacramental teleology that honors Your design for marriage and sexual intimacy, not as ends in themselves but as signs that point beyond themselves to communion, holiness, and love.

As we contemplate the transformative power of sexual intimacy within marriage, may ongoing, grace-filled conversation deepen our union: with You, Our Triune God—Father, Son, and Holy Spirit; with one another as fellow pilgrims in faith; and with ourselves as beloved sons and daughters, created in Your image and redeemed by Your love.

Through Jesus Christ, our Lord and Savior.

Amen.

APPENDIX 2

THE THREE-MINUTE GAME: STRENGTHENING CONNECTION

1. <u>Roles</u>: Two distinct roles exist in the game: the "giver" and the "receiver."

2. <u>Communication</u>: The receiver's task is to convey their comfort level and touch preferences throughout the three minutes. They may respond with a "yes" to certain touches and a "no" to others, or express uncertainties or specific requests.

> There are two questions, each serving as an offer or invitation:
>
> a) "How do you want me to touch you for three minutes?"
>
> b) "How do you want to touch me for three minutes?"
>
> Each person alternates asking these questions, and the agreed-upon actions are then performed.

When you inquire about your partner's desires and receive a response, pause and assess whether you can fulfill it with a wholehearted commitment. Set limits as necessary.

Changing your mind during the activity is allowed, and requesting more than three minutes is acceptable, provided both partners receive equal time.

3. <u>Setting the Tone</u>: Couples can prepare their environment in simple, intentional ways that support the senses and invite connection—such as softening the lighting, reducing distractions, adding music, or choosing textures that feel comfortable. These small acts create a space that feels safe and welcoming, allowing spouses to relax, be present, and enter more easily into intimacy with one another.

4. <u>Setting the Timer</u>: A three-minute timer is used. Throughout this period, the giver provides touch to the receiver, who communicates their boundaries and preferences.

5. <u>Feedback</u>: Following the three-minute interval, a debriefing period usually occurs. During this time, participants share their experiences, lessons learned, and insights gained from the exercise.

APPENDIX 3

TAKING THE NEXT STEPS

Going forward, I intend to establish grace-filled communities—discipleship circles, if you will—to perpetuate this conversation about an alternative approach to sexual wholeness, integrity, and flourishing.[116] I'm strongly convinced that if spouses embrace the principles and teleology proposed above, prioritizing them over the superficiality of techniques and the ideologies of the *Radical No* and *Radical Yes*, they will deepen their connection with themselves, each other, and the Triune God. I envision two approaches for the integration and implementation of purpose-guided pleasure:

> 1. Partner with local faith communities and parishes that wish to support couples utilizing this material for a distinctive dialogue on sexual wholeness, integrity, and flourishing.

> 2. Bring together four to six couples in a more intimate setting, such as a living room, to navigate through the material.

These two approaches might look like the following:

<u>**Seven-Week Discipleship Circle (a facilitated conversation):**</u>

1. Narrative Introduction

2. The *Radical No*

3. The *Radical Yes*

4. Being a "Good Gift"

5. Sacramental Lens

6. Practices and Rituals

7. Concluding Thoughts

<u>**Thursday to Saturday Retreat:**</u>

Thursday Night:
   Opening Session

Friday Morning:
   The Radical No
   The Radical Yes

Friday Afternoon:
   Being a "Good Gift"
   Sacramental Lens

Friday Evening:
   Dinner and Social Time

Saturday Morning:
   Practices and Rituals
   Concluding Session and Next Steps

From this point, it's easy to anticipate that challenges and obstacles may arise. Transitioning from theology proper to everyday theology can be difficult. Therefore, process groups separated by gender will be designed specifically for men and women to address distinct concerns or foster a more tailored support system. Additionally, couple-to-couple mentoring from my spouse and me will be available. All these offerings aim to provide opportunities for further discipleship related to sexuality and to enable individuals to bring their concerns directly to one another and to the Lord.

APPENDIX 4

BIBLICAL TEXTS SHAPING CHRISTIAN VIEWS ON SEXUALITY

<u>I. Marriage as the Divine Framework</u>

Emphasizing the biblical foundation of marital unity and its importance in sexual relationships.

> A. Genesis 2:24–25: "That is why a man leaves his father and mother and is united to his wife, and they become one flesh. Adam and his wife were both naked, and they felt no shame."

> B. Ephesians 5:31: "For this reason, a man will leave his father and mother and be united to his wife, and the two will become one flesh."

<u>II. Purity and Fidelity in Sexual Relations</u>

Understanding the biblical call for faithfulness and purity within marriage. Also, the importance of sexual relations within marriage to avoid sexual immorality.

A. Hebrews 13:4: "Marriage should be honored by all, and the marriage bed kept pure (undefiled), for God will judge the adulterer and all the sexually immoral."

B. 1 Corinthians 6:18: "Flee from sexual immorality."

C. 1 Corinthians 7:1–2: "Now for the matters you wrote about: 'It is good for a man not to have sexual relations with a woman.' But since sexual immorality is occurring, each man should have sexual relations with his own wife, and each woman with her own husband."

III. Mutual Love and Respect

Highlighting the importance of mutual love, respect, and sacrificial love in marital relationships.

A. Ephesians 5:25: "Husbands, love your wives, just as Christ loved the church and gave himself up for her."

B. Ephesians 5:33: "However, each one of you also must love his wife as he loves himself, and the wife must respect her husband."

C. 1 Peter 3:7: "Husbands, in the same way, be considerate as you live with your wives, and treat them with respect..."

D. 1 Peter 3:1: "Wives, in the same way, submit yourselves to your own husbands so that, if any of them do not believe the word, they may be won over without words by the behavior of their wives."

IV. Chastity: Avoiding Lust and Adultery

Recognizing the biblical warning against lust and the importance of maintaining purity of heart.

> A. Matthew 5:27–28: "You have heard that it was said, 'You shall not commit adultery.' But I tell you that anyone who looks at a woman lustfully has already committed adultery with her in his heart."

V. Responsibility and Communication

These passages emphasize the mutual responsibility, selflessness, and need for open communication within the marriage relationship, where both spouses are encouraged to prioritize each other's needs and desires. Guidance for fulfilling marital duties and mutual consent.

> A. 1 Corinthians 7:3–5: "The husband should fulfill his marital duty to his wife, and likewise the wife to her husband. The wife does not have authority over her own body but yields it to her husband. In the same way, the husband does not have authority over his own body but yields it to his wife."

> Advice on avoiding the seduction of adultery and the importance of marital intimacy.

> B. Proverbs 5:15–20: "Drink water from your own

cistern, running water from your own well. Should your springs overflow in the streets, your streams of water in the public squares? Let them be yours alone, never to be shared with strangers. May your fountain be blessed, and may you rejoice in the wife of your youth. A loving doe, a graceful deer—may her breasts satisfy you always, may you ever be intoxicated with her love. Why, my son, be intoxicated with another man's wife? Why embrace the bosom of a wayward woman?"

VI. Moderation and Self-Control

Understanding the biblical call for moderation and self-control in marital intimacy.

> A. 1 Corinthians 7:5: "Do not deprive each other except perhaps by mutual consent and for a time, so that you may devote yourselves to prayer."

VII. God's Grace and Forgiveness

Acknowledging the role of God's grace and forgiveness in the context of marital challenges and mistakes. Grace is the antidote for shame.

> A. 1 John 1:9: "If we confess our sins, he is faithful and just and will forgive us our sins and purify us from all unrighteousness."

Celebrating Marital Intimacy

B. Song of Solomon

This entire book celebrates the beauty and passion of love within marriage. It explores the rich imagery and expressions of love found in the marital embrace and sexual love.

This biblical text portrays the depth of emotional and physical connection within the context of marriage.

While the primary focus is on the romantic and sensual love between a bride and bridegroom, some interpret it as a symbol of the spiritual love relationship between God and humanity, as an allegory of God's passionate and intimate love for His people.

ACKNOWLEDGMENTS

To you, the reader, thank you for taking the time to engage with this work. May it be a blessing to you in your life.

Nothing significant in my life has happened without the support of my wife, Lisa Rose. She has faithfully stood by my side through thick and thin, serving as a steady influence who continually reminds me of all that's good, true, and beautiful in life and love. Our love—our marriage, a true sacramental union—reflects God's redeeming love for us, our family, and the world.

The work you hold in your hands is more than just a thought experiment. It flows from my reflections on those I've served in my counseling practice and as a clinical chaplain to military veterans, as well as from my own lived experience in married life. This project has inspired me, renewed my ministry, and supported my journey of healing and growth in holiness and wholeness.

I am grateful to the many friends and family members who offered encouragement and support throughout this project. I extend particular thanks to my father, Stephen Bennion, for his meticulous proofreading and thoughtful suggestions as a beta reader; his involvement not only strengthened the manuscript but also deepened our friendship, making this collaboration a meaningful chapter in our relationship. I am also thankful to Martha Boehm for her steady encouragement and for checking in along the way, as well as to Claire Dunn for careful proofreading and to Jane Dixon-Smith for her generous design consultation.

I am especially thankful to my doctoral cohort and to Dr. Melissa Snarr, Director of the Doctor of Ministry in Integrative Chaplaincy program at Vanderbilt Divinity School, whose thoughtful leadership, intellectual rigor, and pastoral sensitivity laid a critical foundation for much of the work in these pages. Their guidance challenged and inspired me in ways that continue to influence my vocation and ministry.

Much of what I share here is more inheritance than invention. These reflections come from a lifetime of listening and learning, shaped by Scripture, tradition, and the voices of many teachers, friends, and colleagues whose names I might not remember. If there's wisdom here, it's because I've been fortunate to receive it from others, and I'm thankful to friends near and far whose conversations, encouragement, and presence have refreshed my spirit and contributed in unseen but meaningful ways to this work.

To the many authors, theologians, and practitioners whose work I've cited: while I do not agree with all the views expressed by those I mention, the insights I include have provided meaningful value and have earned their place in this work. I'm grateful for how their contributions have helped clarify the path forward.

Above all, I thank Jesus Christ, who continues to guide me through both wilderness and comfort, and in whom all truth and healing ultimately reside. It is by His grace that I walk this path, and to Him I entrust every word written here and every heart this work may touch.

CHAPTER NOTES

PREFACE

1   Teleology is the explanation of things in terms of their inherent ends or ultimate goals rather than merely their causes. While closely related to *purpose*—the immediate or intended aim of an action—teleology looks beyond human intention to the natural or ultimate fulfillment toward which things are ordered. In this sense, purpose is specific and proximate, whereas teleology is comprehensive and ultimate—though both concern what something is "for." Paraphrased from *The American Heritage Dictionary of the English Language*, 3rd edition (Boston: Houghton Mifflin, 1992), s.v. "teleology," "purpose."

PART I. INTRODUCTION

2   This entails a willingness to suspend current ideas and embrace new practices that foster sexual wholeness, integrity, and flourishing in married life. Ultimately, it offers spouses a sacred space in which to experience profound meaning and purpose in an embodied and intimate way through a sacramental approach to sexual love. Sexual flourishing encompasses the profound Jewish concept of Shalom—wholeness, integrity, soundness, community, connectedness, righteousness, justice, and well-being. These attributes extend to one's relationship with oneself, with one another, and with the Triune God.

1 | A PERSONAL JOURNEY: SETTING THE STAGE

3   Teresa J. Hornsby, "Gender, Sexuality, and the New Testament." VDS Doctor of Ministry Program. October 15, 2021. Video, 41:42. https://vanderbilt.app.box.com/s/nh7939ebt9ojg3o4f2hty7hk8due6uf7/file/873183132075

4   Joseph Smith, *The Book of Mormon: Another Testament of Jesus Christ*, First Edition (Salt Lake City, Utah: The Church of Jesus Christ of Latter-day Saints, 1981).

5   The Church of Jesus Christ of Latter-day Saints, *The Doctrine and Covenants | The Pearl of Great Price* (The Church of Jesus Christ of Latter-day Saints, 2018).

6   Dawne Moon and Theresa W. Tobin, "Sunsets and Solidarity: Overcoming Sac-

ramental Shame in Conservative Christian Churches to Forge a Queer Vision of Love and Justice," *Hypatia* 33, no. 3 (2018): 451–68. https://doi.org/10.1111/hypa.12413

7   For some, the word permissive can have an implied connotation differing from the definitive meaning, and for that reason, I offer a definition of the word permissive from *The American Heritage Dictionary of the English Language*, 3rd edition (Boston: Houghton Mifflin, 1992): "1. Granting or inclined to grant permission; tolerant or lenient. 2. Characterized by freedom of personal behavior or a disregard of traditional social mores."

PART II. CULTURAL CONFLICT

2 | NAVIGATING EXTREMES: RADICAL NO AND RADICAL YES

8   These two expressions—*Radical No* and *Radical Yes*—arose out of a mutual conversation with Dr. Julia Sadusky, author, speaker, and psychologist. https://www.juliasadusky.com

9   The Christian theological view of God (one God in three divine persons—the Father, the Son, and the Holy Spirit), articulated in the historic creeds of the undivided church: the Apostles Creed, the Nicene Creed, and the Athanasian Creed.

10 Douglas Braun-Harvey and Michael A. Vigorito, *Treating Out of Control Sexual Behavior: Rethinking Sex Addiction*, 1st edition (New York: Springer Publishing Company, 2015).

11 Shaunti Feldhahn and Dr Michael Sytsma, *Secrets of Sex and Marriage: 8 Surprises That Make All the Difference* (Minneapolis, Minnesota: Bethany House Publishers, 2023).

3 | THE RADICAL NO: PURITY CULTURE

12 Around the same time, the solidifying changes in gender roles also created a backlash of what it means to be a biblical woman. Debates arose between those referred to as egalitarians and complementarians. Personal conversation with Dr. Melissa Snarr, Vanderbilt Divinity School.

13 J. I. Packer, *Rediscovering Holiness: Know the Fullness of Life with God*, Reissue edition (Ventura, California: Baker Books, 2009).

14 Rachel Joy Welcher and Scott Sauls, *Talking Back to Purity Culture: Rediscovering Faithful Christian Sexuality* (Downers Grove, Illinois: IVP, 2020).

15 Rebecca Lemke, *The Scarlet Virgins: When Sex Replaces Salvation* (Norman, Oklahoma: Anatole, 2017).

16 Laurie Handlers, *Sex & Happiness: The Tantric Laws of Intimacy*, 1st edition (Butterfly Workshops Press, 2007).

17 Laura M. Brotherson, *Knowing HER Intimately: 12 Keys for Creating a Sextraordinary Marriage*, Illustrated edition (Inspire Book, 2016).

18 Rachel Joy Welcher and Scott Sauls, *Talking Back to Purity Culture: Rediscovering Faithful Christian Sexuality* (Downers Grove, Illinois: IVP, 2020).

19 The following example has been modified to protect the privacy of the individuals involved. All identifying information has been removed or changed.

20 Emily Nagoski, *Come As You Are: Revised and Updated: The Surprising New Science That Will Transform Your Sex Life*, Updated edition (New York: Simon & Schuster, 2021).

21 Brotherson, *Knowing HER Intimately*.

22 Barry McCarthy and Emily McCarthy, *Rekindling Desire*, 3rd edition (New York: Routledge, 2019).

23 Shelia Wray Gregoire, *The Great Sex Rescue: The Lies You've Been Taught and How to Recover What God Intended* (Grand Rapids, Michigan: Baker Books, 2021).

24 The following example has been modified to protect the privacy of the individuals involved. All identifying information has been removed or changed.

25 How this phrase is interpreted and applied may vary depending on one's basic beliefs (or worldview), everyday theology, and cultural and/or religious background.

26 Welcher and Sauls, *Talking Back to Purity Culture*.

27   John Eldredge, *Wild at Heart: Discovering the Secret of a Man's Soul* (Nashville, TN: Thomas Nelson, 2001).

28 Tina Schermer Sellers, *Sex, God, and the Conservative Church: Erasing Shame from Sexual Intimacy*. (New York: Routledge, 2017).

29 Teresa J. Hornsby, "Gender, Sexuality, and the New Testament." VDS Doctor of Ministry Program. October 15, 2021. Video, 41:42. https://vanderbilt.app.box.com/s/nh7939ebt9ojg3o4f2hty7hk8due6uf7/file/873183132075

4 | THE RADICAL YES: PERMISSIVE CULTURE

30   For some, the expression "unfettered"—not controlled, limited, or prevented by anyone—may work better. Personal conversation with Dr. Melissa Snarr, Vanderbilt Divinity School.

31   *The American Heritage Dictionary of the English Language*, 3rd edition (Boston: Houghton Mifflin, 1992).

32   *The American Heritage Dictionary of the English Language.*

33   Love Coach Academy Intimacy Training and Certification: Sex and Intimacy in Conscious Relationship. Gabriella Cordova, educator and advocate for sex positivity and healthy sexuality, and founder of Sex-Positive World (https://www.sexpositiveworld.org). This is a paraphrasing of what, to the best of my memory, I recall her saying.

34   Sean McDowell, *Chasing Love: Sex, Love, and Relationships in a Confused Culture* (Brentwood, Tennessee: B&H Books, 2020).

35   Louise Perry, *The Case Against the Sexual Revolution*, 1st edition (Cambridge, UK; Medford, Massachusetts: Polity, 2022).

36   Robert N. (Neelly) Bellah, *Habits of the Heart: Individualism and Commitment in American Life*: Updated Edition with a New Introduction, 1st California paperback edition (Berkeley, California: University of California Press, 1996).

37   Personal conversation with Dr. Melissa Snarr, Vanderbilt Divinity School.

38   Dan Scott, *Naked and Not Ashamed: How God Redeems Our Sexuality* (Eugene, Oregon: Harvest House Publishers, 2008).

39   The following example has been modified to protect the privacy of the individuals involved. All identifying information has been removed or changed.

40   Donna Freitas, *Sex and the Soul: Juggling Sexuality, Spirituality, Romance, and Religion on America's College Campuses*, Revised edition (Oxford, UK; New York: Oxford University Press, 2015).

41   Wade, *American Hookup: The New Culture of Sex on Campus*, Reprint edition (New York: W. W. Norton & Company, 2018).

42   Lisa Wade, *American Hookup: The New Culture of Sex on Campus.*

43   It is the opinion of the author that this demonstrates that consent is necessary but not sufficient.

44 Freitas, *Sex and the Soul.*

45 Many women, in the pursuit of love, engage in sex early in the relationship, often with little to no authentic commitment, only to be disappointed. Similarly, but in a different vein, many men seek intimacy and connection through pornography. Both endeavors separate sex from love. Sex does not equate to love.

46 Christine Emba, *Rethinking Sex: A Provocation* (New York: Sentinel, 2022).

47 Dr Elisabeth Sheff, *When Someone You Love Is Polyamorous: Understanding Poly People and Relationships,* Second printing edition (Portland, Oregon: Thorntree Press, 2016).

48 For reference, some of the schools of thought and practice include sexual shamanism and a practical form of esoteric Tantra.

49 These sexual shamanic and tantric spaces were considered sacred and, as such, drugs and alcohol were not permitted to ensure there was safety and people could freely consent.

50 The following example has been modified to protect the privacy of the individuals involved. All identifying information has been removed or changed.

PART III. FINDING A BALANCED APPROACH

51 Surrendra Gangadean, *Philosophical Foundation: A Critical Analysis of Basic Beliefs* (Lanham, Maryland: UPA, 2008).

52 To be clear, I'm not suggesting that those who are sexually permissive or embrace a polyamorous lifestyle are sexual addicts. Rather, I'm suggesting that the resolution or meaning these folks seek is not to be found where they're looking.

53 The following example has been modified to protect the privacy of the individuals involved. All identifying information has been removed or changed.

54 Simon Blackburn, *The Oxford Dictionary of Philosophy,* 3rd edition (Oxford: Oxford University Press, 2016).

55 The terms "sexual love" and "the marital embrace" are often used interchangeably, although they hold slightly different meanings. "Sexual love" typically refers to the romantic and intimate connection between partners, encompassing emotional and physical intimacy. On the other hand, "the marital embrace" specifically denotes the physical act of sexual intercourse within marriage, symbolizing commitment, love, and unity. ChatGPT, 2024.

56 It's worth noting that the mainline Protestant denomination the United Church of Christ (UCC) and the Unitarian Universalist Association (UUA) faith com-

munity collaborated in the late 1980s to put together a comprehensive lifespan sexuality education curriculum called "Our Whole Lives" (OWL). These faith communities have different theological values from many conservative Christians and even each other. They're seeking to address the gap of knowledge that many youth and adults have in matters related to sexuality.

57 Personal conversation on September 12, 2023, with Sheila Wray Gregoire, speaker and author of *The Great Sex Rescue* (2021), where she highlighted this connection, drawing on her research as well as studies conducted by the University of Toronto.

58 Vaginismus is the involuntary spasm or contraction of the muscles surrounding the vaginal opening, which can make vaginal penetration painful, difficult, or impossible. *American Heritage Dictionary of the English Language*, 3rd edition (Boston: Houghton Mifflin, 1992), s.v. "vaginismus."

59 In particular, I'm thinking of Karol Wojtyla, *Love & Responsibility: New Translation*, trans. Grzegorz Ignatik (Boston, Massachusetts: Pauline Books & Media, 2013), and his later work as Pope John Paul II: *Man and Woman He Created Them: A Theology of the Body*, trans. Michael M. Waldstein (Boston, Massachusetts: Pauline Books & Media, 2006).

60 Fortunately, there are books such as Edward Sri, *Men, Women, and the Mystery of Love: Practical Insights from John Paul II's Love and Responsibility* (Newburyport, Massachusetts: Franciscan Media, 2015) and Christopher West, *Fill These Hearts: God, Sex, and the Universal Longing* (Image, 2013) that make John Paul II accessible everyday theology for those sitting in the pews.

61 Kyle Harper, *From Shame to Sin: The Christian Transformation of Sexual Morality in Late Antiquity* (Cambridge, Massachusetts: Harvard University Press, 2013).

62 Philip Sherrard, *Christianity and Eros* (Denise Harvey, 1995). Not always the most reliable authority on sexual health, St. Augustine, a prominent theological figure in Western Christian thought, appears to adopt a decidedly conservative stance ("No" par excellence) on sexuality due to his challenges in reconciling his previous libertine lifestyle with his subsequent commitment to Christianity, notably wrestling with matters of lust and chastity.

63 Sherrard, *Christianity and Eros.*

64 J. B. Stump and Chad Meister, eds., *Original Sin and the Fall: Five Views* (Downers Grove, Illinois: IVP Academic, 2020).

65 Lust: a state of human fallenness that tainted human desires; an intense longing, particularly a strong sexual craving or passion.

66 This emphasis on virginity, particularly for women, often stemmed from patriarchal structures that sought to control and regulate women's sexuality. The idea of virgin birth, such as in the case of the Virgin Mary, could be interpreted in ways that reinforced the perceived sanctity of virginity and, in some instances, implied a certain negative view of sexual activity. Personal conversation based on feedback from Professor George Schmidt, Vanderbilt Divinity School.

67 For example, two titles by Eastern Orthodox theologians: John Chryssavgis, *Love, Sexuality and the Sacrament of Marriage* (Brookline, Massachusetts: Holy Cross Orthodox Press, 2005) and Paul Evdokimov, *The Sacrament of Love: The Nuptial Mystery in the Light of the Orthodox Tradition*, trans. Anthony P. Gythiel and Victoria Steadman (Crestwood, New York: St. Vladimir's Seminary Press, 1985).

68 John Paul II, *Man and Woman He Created Them: A Theology of the Body*.

69 Examples of this are the following works: Juli Slattery, *God, Sex, and Your Marriage* (Chicago, Illinois: Moody Publishers, 2022) and Dr. Juli Slattery and Gary Thomas, *Rethinking Sexuality: God's Design and Why It Matters* (Colorado Springs, Colorado: Multnomah, 2018). Slattery is the creator of the training curriculum Sexual Discipleship®. In her book *God, Sex, and Your Marriage*, she offers and unpacks not techniques but rather "Four Pillars for a Great Sex Life": faithfulness, intimate knowing, sacrificial love, and passionate celebration.

70 Gary Thomas, *Sacred Marriage: What If God Designed Marriage to Make Us Holy More Than to Make Us Happy?*, Reprint edition (Grand Rapids, Michigan: Zondervan, 2015).

5 | A NEW PATH BEYOND THE EXTREMES

71 This isn't to suggest that sex in marriage is literally restricted to the couple's bed. Spouses are encouraged to cultivate biblical eroticism and erotic playfulness that prioritizes adventure and curiosity.

72 A couple of examples: 1 Corinthians 6:16–20; Ephesians 5:31–32.

73 Jacob Hamman, "Play-Informed Chaplaincy: Building Resilience & Fostering Compassion Satisfaction." VDS Doctor of Ministry Program. September 30, 2021. Video, 48:00. https://Vanderbilt.App.Box.Com/s/Jjkymm64j9es905hz8c-77bel9y00csnf/File/866953937402

74 My appreciation for the idea of good gift(s) has been shaped by two significant experiences: 1) an immersive intensive course I attended in the summer of 2023 at the John Paul II Institute for Studies on the Marriage and Family, titled "John Paul II's Wednesday Catechesis and the Meaning of Human Love," and 2) in-

sights gained from reading a chapter titled "Revealing Christ Through the Gift of Our Bodies" in a book on healing for those who have experienced relational and sexual brokenness: Andrew Comiskey, *Living Waters: Restoring Relational Integrity through the Broken Body of Christ* (Desert Stream Ministries, 2022).

75   St. Thomas Aquinas, *Summa Theologica,* Translated by Fathers of the English Dominican Province, Complete English edition (Westminster, Maryland: Christian Classics, 1981).

76   Sexual love in marriage presents an opportunity to prioritize your spouse's needs and desires above your own, while they reciprocate, allowing you both to serve each other mutually. Note, though, that choosing to be a *good gift* to your spouse sexually does *not* involve permitting them to mistreat you or manipulate you into anything unwanted. Should your spouse ever pressure you into any sexual activity against your will, reach out for support from a trusted friend, mentor, pastor, or counselor.

77   It's crucial to interpret this verse carefully to avoid misapplications that could contribute to dangerous and unhealthy power dynamics. Emphasis should be placed on mutual submission; this is not a one-sided command. Husband and wife are called to submit to each other, which expresses itself in both love and respect. It's prudent for Christian leaders to reinforce this emphasis alongside principles like equality, mutual respect, and love within the intricate framework of marital relationships.

78   Steven R. Tracy, "What Does 'Submit in Everything' Really Mean? The Nature and Scope of Marital Submission," *Trinity Journal* 29, no. 2 (2008): 298–303.

79   Steven R. Tracy, 2008.

80   Sarah Sumner, *Just How Married Do You Want To Be?: Practicing Oneness in Marriage*, 16th edition (ReadHowYouWant, 2012).

81   Balancing self-love with selflessness in relationships involves nurturing one's individual identity while willingly prioritizing the needs and well-being of one's spouse through open and honest communication, shared values, and a mutual commitment to growth and reciprocity.

82   The Greek word for sacrament is μυστήριο (mystērion) or mystery.

83   This description aligns with the principles of soft complementarianism in the context of Christian theology. Complementarianism is a theological view that affirms men and women as equal in the context of marriage and emphasizes distinct but complementary roles for husbands and wives.

84 Anthony Lo Bello, *The Origins of Catholic Words: A Discursive Dictionary* (Washington, D.C.: Catholic University of America Press, 2020).

85 Samuel L. Bray and Drew Nathaniel Keane, eds., *The 1662 Book of Common Prayer: International Edition* (Downers Grove, Illinois: IVP Academic, 2021).

86 John Godfrey Saxe, "'With My Body I Thee Worship.' Anglican Marriage Service" (New York, 1889). John Godfrey Saxe is renowned for his rendition of the Indian parable "The Blind Men and the Elephant."

87 This alludes to "la petite mort," a French expression translating to "the little death" in English, commonly used metaphorically for orgasm or the brief loss of consciousness and physical sensations during sexual climax. The phrase is associated with the French language in the context of romantic or sensual experiences.

88 The sacramental life or sacramental nature of things more broadly spoken about would be true of other nonsexual areas or practices of life as well (e.g., foot washing, communal eating, etc.). Though outside of the scope of this book, it would be reasonable to the sacramental imagination to consider that those who have embraced a vocation of celibacy or find themselves in as state of singleness could also access a sacramental way of living, offering connection to the Holy Other.

6 | SEEING SEX AS SACRED: SACRAMENTAL THINKING

89 It's similar to, though not the same as, the expression to "see with the mind's eye."

90 Samuel L. Bray and Drew Nathaniel Keane, eds., *The 1662 Book of Common Prayer: International Edition* (Downers Grove, Illinois: IVP Academic, 2021).

91 Paul Evdokimov, *The Sacrament of Love: The Nuptial Mystery in the Light of the Orthodox Tradition*, trans. Anthony P. Gythiel and Victoria Steadman (Crestwood, New York: St Vladimir's Seminary Press, 1985); *Catechism of the Catholic Church*, 2nd edition (Vatican City: Libreria Editrice Vaticana, 2000), 320.

92 Bray and Keane, *The 1662 Book of Common Prayer*.

93 Sean McDowell, *Chasing Love: Sex, Love, and Relationships in a Confused Culture* (Brentwood, Tennessee: B&H Books, 2020).

94 "Seeing God w/ Hans Boersma." Holy C of E Podcast Interview. December 14, 2021. https://Open.Spotify.Com/Episode/3DYZzdiSOCGvWemVkGllrS?si=T-B5LOLASSIGZw93m_b-HWw

95 *Catechism of the Catholic Church.*

96 Christopher West, *Theology of the Body for Beginners: Rediscovering the Meaning of Life, Love, Sex, and Gender*, Updated, revised, and expanded edition (North Palm

Beach, Florida: Wellspring, 2018).

97 It's important to emphasize that as spouses embark on this spiritual quest, they'll benefit from recognizing that while their sexual union is a crucial aspect of their bond, it alone doesn't suffice for the profound journey toward a higher, transcendent connection. In other words, their sexual union is a necessary but not sufficient element in their journey.

PART IV. PRACTICAL GUIDANCE FOR CHRISTIAN COUPLES

7 | REDISCOVERING PURPOSE IN PLAYFUL INTIMACY

98 I first heard the expression "erotic playfulness" used by Jennifer Degler, Ph.D., a licensed clinical psychologist, life coach, speaker, and author. https://jenniferdegler.com

99 The Triune God is one divine essence, eternally existing as three distinct Persons—Father, Son, and Holy Spirit—whose very identity is relational. God creates out of this eternal communion and freely enters into relationship with His creation without ceasing to be God. Creation is therefore a pure gift, an overflow of divine love. God creates not to complete Himself but to communicate His goodness and generosity.

8 | FOCUSING ON PURPOSE, NOT JUST TECHNIQUES

100 St. Thomas Aguinas, *Summa Theologica*, translated by Fathers of the English Dominican Province, Complete English edition (Westminster, Maryland: Christian Classics, 1981).

101 Gremlins, in folklore and popular culture, are mischievous mythical creatures known for causing technical malfunctions and disruptions. I'm using them here as a symbolic representation of unpredictable elements that come up in relationship work, specifically the manifestation of trauma responses as unpredictable and disruptive reactions to triggering stimuli. I was first introduced to this idea/image by Isa Jones.

102 At the end of the age, with the consummation of all things, the sign of marriage and sexual love will no longer be needed (Revelation 21). It's for this reason that Jesus says in the Gospels that there will be no marriage.

103 Tim Alan Gardner and Scott M. Stanley, *Sacred Sex: A Spiritual Celebration of Oneness in Marriage*, 1st edition (Colorado Springs, Colorado: WaterBrook, 2002).

9 | ENJOYING RIGHTLY: PLEASURE IN LIGHT OF PURPOSE

104 Tim Alan Gardner and Scott M. Stanley, *Sacred Sex: A Spiritual Celebration of Oneness in Marriage*, 1st edition (Colorado Springs, Colorado: WaterBrook, 2002).

105 As a clinician who integrates mental health and spirituality, I affirm the notion of common grace—the divine goodness and benevolence that God extends to all of humanity, regardless of their faith. This is reflected in God's universal care for His creation, as expressed in Matthew 5:45, where it's stated, "For he (the Father) makes his sun rise on the evil and on the good, and sends rain on the just and on the unjust." With this in mind, the best practices, rites, and rituals herein are from various practitioners. This decision is not an explicit endorsement or support for the entirety of their bodies of work.

106 Rich Villodas and Pete Scazzero, *The Deeply Formed Life: Five Transformative Values to Root Us in the Way of Jesus*, Reprint edition (Colorado Springs, Colorado: WaterBrook, 2021).

107 Debra Hirsch and Gabe Lyons, *Redeeming Sex: Naked Conversations About Sexuality and Spirituality* (Downers Grove, Illinois: IVP, 2015).

108 Sandra L. Glahn and C. Gary Barnes, eds., *Sanctified Sexuality: Valuing Sex in an Oversexed World*, Illustrated edition (Grand Rapids, Michigan: Kregel Academic, 2020); Rudolf Otto, *The Idea of the Holy*, trans. John W. Harvey, 2nd edition (London, UK: Oxford University Press, 1958).

10 | INTEGRATING THE SACRED AND PHYSICAL

109 I first learned about this practice from Laurie Handlers, a sex and relationship coach and educator, who learned about it from Margot Anand. Margot Anand and M. E. Naslednikov, *The Art of Sexual Ecstasy: The Path of Sacred Sexuality for Western Lovers* (Jeremy P. Tarcher, 1989).

110 I first encountered the expression "radical generosity" as applied to marriage in *The 80/80 Marriage*, which frames marital love as a movement beyond scorekeeping and notions of fairness toward freely chosen self-giving. Nate Klemp and Kaley Klemp, *The 80/80 Marriage: A New Model for a Happier, Stronger Relationship* (New York: Penguin Books, 2021).

111 Appendix 2 provides an overview of the Three-Minute Game, primarily in the developer's own words as presented in *The Art of Receiving and Giving* by Betty Martin and Robyn Dalzen (Luminare Press, 2021) and adapted with some clarifying notes from my own work with the practice as a clinician.

112 Ramsay, Ruth, "Revamp Your Sex Life in 6 Minutes." TEDx Talks. July 11, 2023. Video, 6:36. https://www.youtube.com/Watch?v=I-3CANRKuAM

11 | EMBRACING HEALING VS. ONLY SEEKING SOLUTIONS

113 Bruce T. Morrill, *Divine Worship and Human Healing: Liturgical Theology at the Margins of Life and Death* (Collegeville, Minnesota: Liturgical Press, 2009).

114 Megan Lara Negendank and Stephanie Buehler, *Loving Someone Who Has Sexual Trauma: A Compassionate Guide to Supporting Your Partner and Improving Your Relationship*, 1st edition (Oakland, California: New Harbinger Publications, 2023); Staci Haines, *Healing Sex: A Mind-Body Approach to Healing Sexual Trauma*, 2nd edition (San Francisco, California: Cleis Press, 2007).

12 | FINAL REFLECTIONS AND ENCOURAGEMENT

115 See Appendix 1 for my closing Benediction.

APPENDIX 3: TAKING THE NEXT STEPS

116 The expression *discipleship circle* I first heard from Francie Winslow, host of *Heaven in Your Home* podcast.

ABOUT THE AUTHOR

Scott Bennion, **D.Min., BCPC, ABS,** is a board-certified pastoral counselor and clinical chaplain, as well as a certified sexologist, a whole health coach, and a spiritual director. He serves in private practice and as a chaplain with the U.S. Department of Veterans Affairs.

His work is rooted in a Christian worldview, integrating faith and mental health with faith-centered support for sexual intimacy and relationship wellness, and attending to the deep longing of the human heart for wholeness and communion. With pastoral wisdom and deep respect for each person's story, Scott helps others move toward greater healing, wholeness, and a deeper connection with God, themselves, and those they love. He lives in Phoenix, Arizona, with his wife, Lisa Rose.

Learn more at faithloveandsexuality.com

PERSONAL REFLECTIONS AND PRAYER